TAKE YOUR
FRAMEWORK
AND STICK
IT UP YOUR
PIPELINE

Finding a new normal
in business

Hugh Marquis

ENDORSEMENTS

"What a great book! Within the pages of Hugh Marquis's *Take Your Framework and Stick It Up Your Pipeline*, you'll find strong principles of kingdom business. But, because they are God-given, these insights are applicable in every arena of life. Marquis writes about healthy leadership, creating a vision, launching people into their destinies, and empowering others to soar. These are values we absolutely need in our businesses, but they are also necessary for our schools, our communities, and our families. This book is transformational, written by a man who has allowed God to crack open his heart, speak into areas of brokenness, and cast vision not only into his business but also his identity. Take these lessons and run with them. They are brilliant, generous, and designed for reformation."

Bill Johnson, Bethel Church, Redding, CA, author of *The Way of Life* and *Raising Giant-Killers*

"Hugh and Jane are personal friends who do kingdom business extraordinarily well. They brilliantly practise what they speak about. Hugh invites the reader to do their own deep thinking regarding doing business and running organisations. He offers keen insight with a fresh perspective on a kingdom economy mindset. He looks to change a fear-based business culture towards outrageous favour. *Take Your Framework and Stick It Up Your Pipeline* gives a very honest look at Hugh's journey in business and walking it out with God by saying, 'yes'."

Heidi Baker, PhD, Co-founder and Chairman of the Board, Iris Global

"So many times, God builds us like a ship, from the outside in. First the hull and then the intricacies for what the ship is meant to carry. Hugh Marquis is a man on a voyage. A voyage to take as many business leaders into the redefinition of success that he can carry. Through the annals of his own personal transformation, he will introduce you to a tested process to move into a true identity as a child of God into a clarity of purpose for changing the world. I'm excited to recommend to you *Take Your Framework and Stick It Up Your Pipeline* as you board this Argosy for what God has for you!"

Danny Silk, President of Loving on Purpose, author of *Business of Honor, Keep Your Love On* and *Culture of Honor*

"There are thousands of books in today's market on building, creating and managing businesses. I have read hundreds of them. The essence of these books are similar: create a business plan, make it unique, put in place your systems, market well and knock out your competition, so you succeed. This is business the 'world's way'. While this way of doing business has some merit, what if there was a different way?

Is there a way that 'makes a significant difference' to your life, your business, the people around you and the wider community? A way that significantly prospers you, others and ultimately builds God's Kingdom. When we execute 'HIS Way' of doing business, something incredible takes place; we go beyond our natural abilities and tap into God's Supernatural Economy.

This is not theory; these principles work. I am a personal testimony to this. I made millions running companies the world's way, lost it all. Second time around, we have moved back into making millions – 'God's Way'. Not so I can boast or have faster cars, but so I can boast of God and build His Kingdom on Earth. This time around, I am fulfilled, happy, at peace and loving life. What were the keys that transformed my personal, professional and financial life? They were many of the principles that Hugh eloquently expounds in this book.

Hugh is an incredible man of God, a great friend and inspiration to many. I have had the privilege of teaching these principles with Hugh and seen the incredible impact it has had on many lives in Australia and internationally. Now, these same keys can be accessed for a fraction of the price in this incredible and refreshing book.

If you want a book that challenges, inspires and equips you to succeed by trading God's Way, this book is for you!"

David Leslie, Kingdom Investors, www.kingdominvestors.com.au

"Hugh Marquis has written an excellent book which leads the reader into a journey of wealth creation with a purpose. It shows that to be truly successful in business, it is best to start with the end goal in mind. You will learn that by discovering the purpose of your business, it will impact not only how you do business but, more importantly, how you live life. The WHY of your work will lead you to WHAT to do and HOW and make life richer in every way for everyone your business touches. I highly recommend it!"

Stacey Campbell, wesleystaceycampbell.com, beaherointernational.org

"Whenever I go to buy a book, I'm always more curious initially about the author than the book itself. After all, a book is at the end of the day, the extension of the personality, experiences and beliefs of the person writing it. I want to know who they are at home or in their home town, what have they built, is there something to show for all that they are espousing?

I have had the great honour of not only meeting Hugh Marquis but also seeing him in action and experiencing the evidence of what he has built through his business enterprises. This book is written in such a way that Hugh's personality is deeply embedded in the writing style without someone over editing to the point of making it all polish and no punch.

I think many people toy with the idea of being business people and especially kingdom business people. Hugh's dynamic principles and transparent stories will challenge the reader to consider if they are just playing with the idea of being God's businessperson or if they are for real.

Take Your Framework and Stick It Up Your Pipeline will, I believe, inspire you and slap you at the same time, which is exactly what most of us need to become the champions that God has called us to be!"

David Balestri, Executive Business Coach, www.marketplaceinvasion.com.au

"I have had the great honour of ministering and doing life with Hugh Marquis for many years. He is full of wisdom, discernment and carries a tremendous prophetic grace. Hugh and his amazing wife Jane have blessed me by the way they carry the character of Jesus and the love for the Kingdom of God in the marketplace. In his book *Take Your Framework and Stick It Up Your Pipeline* you will not only discover the story of a man and his business, but you will also uncover golden nuggets of practical truth and profound revelation from the Lord that will change your mindset and minister to your heart.

I was deeply moved by Hugh's transparency and willingness to share his life experiences and personal testimonies throughout this book. If you have a call to business, a passion for the marketplace or the local church, this book is guaranteed to encourage you and give you a fresh perspective for your life's purpose and business.

I'm thankful that Hugh and Jane have been willing to be obedient and passionate about their calling, and I am proud of my friend for writing this brilliant book!"

David Wagner, Fathers Heart Ministries, Franklin, Tennessee USA

"This book is not rocket science, and Hugh Marquis is not perfect. That's what makes this book great! If it presented processes that only a few could master, it would be irrelevant. If Hugh was some elite individual, it's immediately out of reach, and neither of these is true.

Certainly, the principles for many ARE a paradigm shift that will create a level of discomfort, but they herald a different way of life and business that are literally world-changing if you are prepared to listen to the still small voice – read it, read it again and apply it – it will change your future."

Drew Gormlie, Senior Pastor, Life! Central, CEO, L'Arte Central and HelpNet

"In this inspiring read, Hugh Marquis shows us how kingdom business can look different to corporate greed or even common 'best practice'. Teaching by example, Hugh uses his own journey from insecure visionary to authentic collaborator to 'flip' the way we look at business. If economics is the study of scarce resources, 'kingdomnomics' is an exploration of abundance.

What happens when a community of businesses seek to complete, rather than compete? When they are all helping each other to win at the same time as encouraging every stakeholder to find and live his or her purpose? The focus of business moves from 'getting' to 'healing', and business suddenly starts to transform communities, cities and nations.

I have an MBA, have run several businesses and now help to lead a bible college, but I am always looking to learn. I'm inspired by Hugh's invitation to be a 'kingdompreneuer', and I am certain you will find this book inspiring too."

Nathan Bailey, Principal, Stairway College, Director, Simplify Solutions

"In *Take Your Framework and Stick It Up Your Pipeline* Hugh Marquis lays to rest the myth that businesses only exist for the benefit of the shareholders. What makes this book so compelling is that the insights it contains work. *Take Your Framework and Stick It Up Your Pipeline* is a valuable field manual for all who long to put their money where their mouth is and see their business realise its potential to be the force for good that God intended. Well done Hugh!"

Arleen Westerhof, PhD, Founder and Executive Director, Economic Summit

"I've known Hugh for a long time. Over the years, I've been with him in good times and not so good, and I've watched him in very difficult situations and under enormous pressure. He continually amazes me with his incredible resilience and his will to understand the underlying circumstances and causes and learn from them. As you read the pages of this book, you will get a peek into his inspiring journey, his conclusions, and a comprehensive roadmap to what real success looks like. Furthermore, I believe reading this book has the capability to accelerate many of us into a life of low regret."

David Drake, Founder, Revelation Software Concepts

"While Hugh classifies this as a business book – it's really not. Certainly Hugh's life experience in business is a big part of what he shares, but this is a challenge book. You have probably already figured out from the title – Hugh likes to push you. He will make you a little uncomfortable if you let him. Hugh lives this stuff!

My wife and I are honored to call Hugh a friend and brother. His passion for radical transformation in the role business must play in society will make you examine your own approach. He thinks big – not just a business strategy or an idea but fundamentally how do we live our lives in a way that will change a nation's economy and the opportunities for its most vulnerable members. The rules must change if we want to see real change in people's lives.

So dive in – what if each of us tried a different approach? Maybe we should not read the same old stuff and hope it gets better. I think you might get a 'bug' if you examine your thoughts as Hugh leads you through these pages."

Neal E Arnold, Chief Executive Officer and President, SunflowerBank, Neal.Arnold@SunflowerBank.com

"I have the great privilege of counting Hugh and Jane as my friends. To know them is to see power, love and wisdom in action. When you live in the realm of abundance like Hugh, you realise who and what you have access to. *Take Your Framework and Stick It Up Your Pipeline* is a must read for anyone that is looking for what you can do FROM God not just for God.

The marketplace is being redeemed and reclaimed as ordinary people start to do extraordinary things with their lives.

The kingdom principles by a kingdom-possessed entrepreneur will take you on a journey of a life that will flourish.

Thank you Hugh for helping me and thousands of others on a path to reach our full potential."

Leif Hetland, President, Global Mission Awareness, Author, Giant Slayers

Scripture quotations marked TPT are from The Passion Translation®. Copyright © 2017, 2018 by Passion & Fire Ministries, Inc. Used by permission. All rights reserved. ThePassionTranslation.com.

Scripture quotations taken from the New American Standard Bible® (NASB), Copyright © 1960, 1962, 1963, 1968, 1971, 1972, 1973, 1975, 1977, 1995 by The Lockman Foundation. Used by permission. www.Lockman.org

Scripture quotations marked (NLT) are taken from the Holy Bible, New Living Translation, copyright © 1996, 2004, 2015 by Tyndale House Foundation. Used by permission of Tyndale House Publishers, Inc., Carol Stream, Illinois 60188. All rights reserved.

ISBN: 978-1-925921-73-1

Project management and text design by Michael Hanrahan Publishing
Cover design by Jake Leenheers

Contents

Acknowledgements

This book has been over eight years in the making. God challenged me to write it in 2011. He gave me the title *Take Your Framework and Stick It Up Your Pipeline*, and told me to write a book about how to build businesses differently. Simple enough. I began to write, but then the doubts overwhelmed me like a flood. Why should people listen to me? If they really knew who I was and what I'd done – why would they listen to a word I had to say? I put the whole idea on the shelf and got on with life. My sense of unworthiness drowned out God's direction.

After working through many of my issues, I picked up the book and began writing again. A fresh wave of doubts swamped me! Who would publish anything I wrote? Who would buy it? Why would my book make a difference when there are thousands of business books gathering dust on shelves or languishing in e-book libraries on smartphones around the world? Yep, I put it back on the shelf.

Then I felt God saying that I needed to write it because it was a practical guide, with steps for how He wants to change the world. That scared me! Actually, I was terrified. Why me? There are plenty of others far more qualified to write and speak on such things. But He didn't let up. Then Jane, my amazing wife, started asking, "Well, when are you going to do something about the book?"

Which brings me to my incredible family. On February 14, 1987, Jane said "I do" to me. It was in sickness and health, for richer or poorer, in good times and bad and we have had all of those and some. Without Jane, this journey would not have half its stories. Jane continues to be my support, my friend, my everything. I was given some great marriage advice from a friend, "Don't marry someone you want to spend the rest of your life with, marry someone you can't live the rest of your life without". Jane, you are that someone.

To my three children Breanne, Savannah, and Owen, I am very proud of each of you and, though completely different, you light up my life. Thank you for giving me lots of ammunition for this book.

In my years with God, I've noticed that even though we may have great success, we humans hold up His plans because we don't act when He speaks. While I've said yes to God in every other area of my life, I was pretty much saying "No" in this instance. I also think that God can arrange circumstances that allow other things to fall away until we come face to face with what He's asking us to do. That's what happened to me. I finally had to answer the question, "Am I going to write the book?" This time I said "Yes."

The challenge with me writing a book is the same as the challenge I had at school. I didn't like writing generally, and I especially didn't like writing essays because my brain works differently than most people's. The average brain formulates thoughts at 1,000-3,000 words per minute. When my mind is fully functioning, I think at 3,500-4,000 words per minute. I speak at around 900 words per minute with bursts up to 1,200. But I write at about thirty words a minute! This makes staying on any topic long enough to get it on paper nearly impossible! I had to find a different way of doing things and came up with the idea of being interviewed.

What I've loved about this process is that it's been a real example of what it looks like to live in the kingdom of God. We each have our unique part to play. I've been helped immensely by others who embraced their role in the writing of this book, and the telling of my story.

I want to acknowledge and thank Hannah Easton, who dreamed with me about what the book was going to look like. Her wisdom, insight and advice have been invaluable. Many thanks also go to Kim Miatke, who spent time interviewing me in loud restaurants, drawing stories out of me in preparation for the writing of the manuscript. A big thank you to Grace Bailey, who not only started the process of turning the interviews into a written format but also helped me process the reason for and purpose of this book.

It was after the initial process that Renée Geddes stepped into our world. I was at church when a friend asked, "So, how is your book going?" I explained the process and told them I was looking for someone to help me write it. "Why don't you speak to Renée?" they suggested.

I did. I spoke with Renée about what that would look like. We embarked on a journey, with her taking the initial interviews, random thoughts and ideas and bringing order, form and language. We would sit down for coffee, and she would elicit more ideas by asking questions. Renée helped me slow down and articulate the concepts and my experiences. She gently encouraged me in the process and didn't think all my ideas were crazy!

Without others, this would still be an idea sitting on a shelf whose time would never have come. Without Hannah, Kim and Grace, I wouldn't have known where to start. Without Renée, I wouldn't have been able to complete it. We have all played our part. My prayer is that this book would be a useful tool that makes a positive difference in your life, your family, your business, your community and beyond.

I share this with you as an encouragement. I know that there will be many of you who have a 'crazy' idea or dream or word from God and the obstacles have appeared like mountains on the path before you. Maybe it's time to think outside of the usual paradigms and give it a go. If you have a passion, a project that is burning within you; if you have a word from God, don't dismiss it as impossible because while it may be impossible for you, all things are possible with Him. It may simply be that you need others to walk with you, as I did, contributing their skills and passion to the project.

What have you got to lose by giving it a go?

Foreword

I have had the privilege of walking with Hugh as his friend, pastor, mentor and coach. We sat together and prayed God's life into Network Neighborhood when it was a dream in Hugh's heart, and before it became a multi-million-dollar business. I remember standing at Venice station, in Italy, counselling Hugh over the phone when he and Jane separated for a time. We fought together in prayer for the healing of one of their daughters from a brain tumour. I recall the first time Hugh accompanied me to Cambodia and the way he was deeply moved as the Lord moved Hugh's heart to participate in restoring that nation. I was honoured when Hugh sought wisdom from me around the relational tensions in his business that had been created by his blind spots.

We have experienced a lot of life together.

As you read *Take Your Framework and Stick It Up Your Pipeline*, you can be assured that the advice, lessons and wisdom offered have been forged in the realities of life. They have come from Hugh's commitment "to owning his stuff". Hugh knows that a foundational principle for personal growth and organisational culture change is the ability to embrace self-awareness and personal responsibility. This principle can only be fully expressed in the context of loving and life-giving relationships. It underpins who we are becoming and all we accomplish in life, which is an overflow of who we are.

Hugh believes in your potential to make the world a better place and is assured that this belief is at the heart of the culture of the Kingdom of God. To this end, we find Jesus teaching us to care for people as our priority as He commanded us to: "love one another, as I have loved you." Paul, in 1 Timothy, represents this mandate when he writes: "The goal of our instruction is love from a pure heart, from a good conscience and from a sincere faith." To live this lifestyle 24/7 is the great call on, and privilege of, followers of Jesus. We do this by learning how to walk with God, building a life through design not living by default, and by implementing what God holds dear.

My friend Hugh Marquis in *Take Your Framework and Stick It Up Your Pipeline*, shows how to be this type of Kingdom person as he shares vulnerably, openly, boldly and frankly from his own experiences. That is a person who has a personal and corporate culture that begins to reflect Heaven on Earth. While I agree with Hugh that he is 'a work in progress', I admire and applaud his journey that has captured the essence of the saying: 'If not you, who? If not now, when?"

You will be inspired, empowered and challenged to be the best you possible in the here and now, as you join with an army of lovers of Jesus who want to advance His Kingdom in every area of their lives...including business.

Peter McHugh
Senior Minister, Stairway Church Whitehorse,
Melbourne

Introduction

My name is Hugh Marquis, and I'm here to share my story with you. It happened, and it's ongoing. It's not a parable; though there are lessons to learn and I'm still learning them. Had I not walked this path I probably wouldn't believe it, and if you don't believe it, that's ok. But if you will stick with me through the pages of this book, I know that there are nuggets that will set you, your family, your organisation, and your community on a trajectory to change the world around you for the better.

In case you're now wondering what you've gotten yourself into – this is a business book. However, it's not your usual business book. I'm going to share my journey in business, but more importantly, it's my journey with God. I can't talk about business without Him because, without Him, there would be no business to speak of. I've never been one to beat around the bush. I have a reputation for telling it like it is (or at least as I see it), and what I'm going to share with you is the reality of doing business in the kingdom of God. These are the possibilities, and I think they should be the rule, not the exception.

I'm excited to share my experiences; the highs, the lows, the lessons, and to give you practical ways of working in your organisation that will enhance productivity, creativity and your bottom line. If that's all you take away, it will significantly benefit you, your business, your staff and your clients.

However, it will fall short, and I want you to have it all, and so does God!

In the end, I could tell you that my business success comes from my financial knowledge, my commitment to excellence, my approach to releasing my workers, and so on. While all of these factors contribute to the outworking of my businesses, my plans and accompanying steps are ordered and directed by God. My part has primarily been that of saying "Yes", stepping out in faith, committing finances to the vision and being faithful to walk it out.

THE 'WHY' BEHIND MY 'WHAT'

After building and running successful (and the occasional not so successful) businesses for over 30 years, I hired marketing people to help me with my branding. They were well qualified and well-intentioned, attempting to build a brand around whom they thought I was or should be. It was during this process that I had an "Aha!" moment. I realised that I am me. I am the me that God created me to be. I am not a specific name, not a particular title. I have a unique, diverse and unconventional background that has provided me with the skills and opportunities to live and learn the art of business. We are each called to be ourselves; the people we were designed to be, and that the world ultimately needs us to be. We are not what we do. What we accomplish should be the overflow of who we are, and that is all the branding we need.

I grew up in Drysdale and later, the seaside town of Queenscliff on Victoria's Bellarine Peninsula. In my teens, I watched my mother manage a successful, award-winning hotel, but what impressed me most and stayed with me was her servant attitude. She instilled this same attitude in her staff as she served not only her customers but those who worked for her. She knew that without customers, the business would not exist; but without her staff, the customers wouldn't come. She appreciated her employees, and she taught them to value customers by giving them an outstanding experience every time they walked through the door.

I started out working for the opposition (they paid better than family!) and was taught to serve and look after people, wait tables, clean and cook. I have run restaurants, bars, and a French bakehouse. I've built and renovated houses, written computer software, worked in finance, built IT service businesses and developed multimillion-dollar enterprises all around the world. I've owned and directed food companies, manufacturing plants, forestry companies, and run non-profits fighting trafficking and slavery in Cambodia.

I've eaten with the leaders of countries and dined with the poorest of the poor around the world. I've cried with the down and out and celebrated with the victorious. I've had my heart broken by social injustice and had a hand up from those I would consider the neediest. I've led strategic panels and executed business plans. I've helped build better businesses and had the privilege of travelling to over 90 countries, experiencing other cultures and seeing firsthand how we impact each other through trade and relationship, be it for good or ill.

I have been criticised, ridiculed, encouraged and applauded, often for the same thing and at the same time, and I've learnt that it's a matter of perspective. I love to teach, train and equip people to help them achieve their best and launch them into a bright and prosperous future.

I love spending time with people and investing in their world. I believe we live in unprecedented times and the opportunities to bring real and lasting benefit to those who need it most have never been more exciting. The world is becoming smaller, and instead of tearing things down, it is time we work together for the good of all.

In the end, life is about relationships. It's about making the world a better place for having you in it. It's about valuing people who are made in the image of God and releasing them to be all that He created them to be. It's about giving opportunities for people to step up into their identity in God and run with their passion. That's how we transform business culture, and transformed business cultures transform their communities, cities, nations and the world.

Do this, and the bottom line will take care of itself. When people are valued, they will appreciate your business. They will take ownership of your vision, mission, and bottom line and make it their mission to see it come to pass. We have assumed the worst of people. We make the exception the rule. It's time to go from fear to outrageous favour.

WHO SHOULD READ THIS BOOK?

Everyone! Seriously, while this book focusses on organisational culture and change, the principles work anywhere there is a relationship because, in the end, everything worth anything in life comes down to relationships and how we invest in each other.

Whether you are a brand-new start-up operating out of your garage or an established business with two-hundred employees, there is something for everyone willing to go on the journey of transformation. It's time we challenge the status quo driven by greed, fear and corruption and build organisations that care for people as much as they care for profits.

HOW TO READ THIS BOOK

The best way to read this book is from start to finish! However, you can read any of the chapters in isolation and get insight that will help you navigate your way from good to better, better to best with your organisation.

If you're inspired to make or even suggest change within your business, you can grab a bunch of copies and work through the book again with your colleagues and co-workers. Alternatively, maybe you don't own the company you work for and would like to give the book to your boss for Christmas! Trust me; they will thank you! I know that I would have appreciated it!

I know the steps laid out in this book work. I've lived them. I've also made plenty of mistakes along the way so that you don't have to! There is a better way to do business, and it's a way that benefits people, not just in your immediate circle of influence, but in the lives of people you may never meet.

WHAT ARE WE GOING TO COVER?

As I said earlier, I want you to come away from this book with a fresh perspective and practical steps that you can put into action within your organisation. I want you to be able to have great conversations with the people in your business about your vision, mission and higher purpose that inspire them to consider their legacy and purpose.

CHAPTER ONE: WHAT'S THE PURPOSE OF BUSINESS?

Why did any of us go into business in the first place when fifty-one per cent of companies fail within the first five years? It all comes down to vision. What's your vision and is it big enough to get you through the tough times? Find out how to create a legacy that will launch your business into the stratosphere and on the adventure of a lifetime.

CHAPTER TWO: THE NETWORK NEIGHBORHOOD STORY

I started Network Neighborhood (NN) in 1999. The lessons learned in establishing, building and running this multi-million-dollar company were the geneses for this book. It was as I led Network Neighborhood that God taught me how to run a business based on kingdom principles and with a kingdom economy mindset.

CHAPTER THREE: IDENTITY, SELF-AWARENESS AND LEADERSHIP

What does your identity have to do with any of it? Everything! We all see the world through the filters of personality, upbringing and the experiences that shaped us. Learning how to lead and release others authentically is key to living in a culture of honour, vulnerability and transparency.

CHAPTER FOUR: FAILURE AND SUCCESS

What does it mean to fail? What does it mean to succeed? Who decides what they are and how do we define them in our businesses? To what extent has a toxic business culture of greed, fear and corruption defined them for us, and how do we flip the culture? Learn how to create success pathways for your company, staff and clients.

CHAPTER FIVE: UNLOCKING AND UNLEASHING UNTAPPED RESOURCES

Discovering, unlocking and unleashing the potential of ourselves and our employees sounds like a beautiful, life-affirming thing to do. But what does it look like practically and how does it work in the day-to-day running of your business? Learn how to call up the gold in your team, unlock their creativity, and unleash them on an unsuspecting world!

CHAPTER SIX: SURVIVOR'S GUIDE TO RIDING THE WAVE

If we measure success by the financial bottom line of our organisation, we can be taken out by it! In this chapter, we look at the red flags, red herrings and pitfalls of success and why it's crucial that we are clear on our definition of success. When we are clear on our vision, mission and the bigger picture, we'll be able to ride the wave and create longevity. We also revisit 'failure' and 'success' and talk about how to re-fire and re-start when things don't go according to plan.

Next, we dive in and ask, "What happens when it all hits the fan?" You've put your heart and soul into making the transition from a culture of fear to one of favour, and suddenly there's resistance. More than that, it looks like things are falling apart; relationships strain, and there are more misunderstandings than you can poke a stick at. The attack seems to come from all sides. It's all part of the process and can be the making of you, your staff and your business.

CHAPTER SEVEN: THERE'S A WHOLE WORLD WAITING!

It's a big world out there, and it needs you! We don't live or run our organisations in a vacuum. Being in business means that we are blessed with the opportunity to make a difference in the lives of others in our families, businesses, communities, nations and beyond.

CHAPTER EIGHT: THE NEXT STEPS

We come to the end of our journey together and the beginning of lifelong adventures, if we choose to embrace the risk and trust in God. We discuss the next steps and dare to dream bigger than ever before. With Him, the path is from glory to glory. There will always be trials and tribulation, that's life, but when we have the view of Heaven, anything is possible!

THE BOTTOM LINE

Each chapter ends with 'The Bottom Line'. It's a moment for you to stop and think about your business. I want you to come away from each chapter with a fresh perspective and ideas to launch you into the next phase of changing the culture of your organisation and ultimately, the world around you.

ACTION STEPS

In 'Action Steps,' we get practical. We ask questions, provide you with exercises, and give you strategies that will launch your business into a new era of outrageous favour!

Are you ready?

Let's begin!

CHAPTER ONE

What's the purpose of business?

Let's start by stopping for a moment. I want you to consider this question, "What is the purpose of business?" What's the first thing that popped into your head? Was it why you started in business or the reasons you continue to turn up every day? Sit for a bit and ponder it some more, "What is the purpose of business?" or to put it another way, "What is the ultimate reason that businesses exist?"

I believe that business is ultimately here to prosper and provide for the welfare of the whole of society. It has been said that the measure of a civilised society is the care it provides for its most vulnerable members and I think that we as business owners and leaders are perfectly positioned to be the answer to a world in need.

I want us to start our journey by questioning and even challenging the fundamentals of business and the accompanying culture. Why? Because unless we begin at the beginning, it's almost impossible to consider that there could be another way of doing the business of business.

Our collective, accepted 'why' has driven companies, small and large, to operate in ways that produce 'winners' and 'losers', 'successes' and 'failures' – with no thought that we are cheating ourselves out of a way that lifts us all and sets people free.

Back to our question. Do a quick Google search, and you'll discover that even linking the words "purpose" and "business" is fraught! The common denominator in most answers is at the crux of our collective 'why'. They overwhelmingly start with a version of, "to make a profit for those with a stake in the company...be they owners or stakeholders."

I know I'm simplifying, but my point is this; economics and the pursuit of profit are at the core of business culture. Don't get me wrong – business should be profitable – but it's our 'why' that feeds our 'what', 'how' and 'who', and for millions of people across the world, through multiple generations, our collective 'why' has led to untold misery and hardship.

Gordon Gekko's infamous speech in the movie *Wall Street*, based on an address given by the real-life inside trader Ivan Boesky, hit a nerve because it dared to say what we were all secretly thinking;

"The point is, ladies and gentlemen, that greed – for lack of a better word – is good.

Greed is right. Greed works. Greed clarifies, cuts through, and captures the essence of the evolutionary spirit. Greed, in all of its forms – greed for life, for money, for love, knowledge – has marked the upward surge of mankind. And greed – you mark my words – will not only save Teldar Paper, but that other malfunctioning corporation called the USA." (Stone, 1987)

One (of many) problems with this thinking is the notion that 'greed' works in isolation and is a tool to be picked up and used for the benefit of those clever enough to wield it. The reality is that greed has a couple of nasty bedfellows called 'fear' and 'corruption'. If I had to sum them up in one word, it would be 'pride'.

Greed, fear and corruption are the silent partners of the current business culture. For some people, they overtly inform their decision-making processes. Others make decisions based in reaction to the greed, fear and corruption that assaults them daily. Business owners feel coerced into behaving in ways towards others, both inside and outside their companies, that go against the grain and perpetuate the 'winners and losers' narrative widely accepted as part of the cost of doing business.

A DIFFERENT WAY

I want to propose a different way. It's radical in its simplicity, and you may be tempted to dismiss it entirely but let me ask you to keep an open mind. Why? Because IT WORKS! It's working for more and more businesses and communities around the world. I have first-hand experience in business venture after business venture and have benefited from the positive outworking for my employees, clients, suppliers, myself and my family.

What I am proposing is the opposite of greed, fear and corruption, or 'pride'. It's a generous mindset with caring, sharing and prosperity for all which I sum up as 'righteousness'. It's about doing the right thing at the right time for the right reason. When 'pride' is our primary motivator – we will act in ways that produce and promote greed, fear and corruption. When 'righteousness' is our cornerstone – we will make decisions that embody generosity, caring, sharing and prosperity for our community and us.

When we refuse to participate in the toxic culture of greed, fear and corruption that drives much of what we call 'free trade' or the 'free market economy', and instead choose to look after the welfare of others – valuing people above profit – things change.

We are connected as never before. Every aspect of life, from the internet to travel, is bringing the world to our doorstep and sending us to theirs. We can't pretend that what we do in our local business has no ripple effect. Our decisions find their out-working in the communities of others. Whether it's our choice of suppliers, providers, clients, shareholders, employees, friends and family – the ripple extends well beyond the reaches of our small ponds.

This book is devoted to giving you the tools and processes you need to transform your business, taking it from fear and launching you into outrageous favour!

COMPETING VS COMPLETING

We've been taught that the economy is like a pie and that it's finite. That means that if someone else gets a piece of the pie, I miss out and I may as well take my knife and fork and go home!

When we operate in a toxic culture that's rooted in pride – we will inevitably put our interests above everything and everyone else. Our decisions will be fear based and self-protective. It's all about perspective. When we let fear dominate, we become blinkered in our perception – unable to see another way.

How are you doing so far? Still with me? Let me share a story with you to illustrate my point.

A TALE OF TWO FLORISTS

Once upon a time, there were two florists. These two florists had stores at opposite ends of the same street in the centre of town.

The first florist specialised in roses. Their roses were the most fragrant, sumptuous blooms to be found in the city and they had a reputation for exquisite floral arrangements. The second florist specialised in tulips. They and their tulips were the talk of the town for the vivid and vibrant array of colours and the helpfulness of the staff in choosing the right bouquet for any occasion.

One day a stranger wandered into the first florist's shop. They were new in town and keen to discover the delights of the main street. After exchanging pleasantries, the stranger asked if they had any tulips for sale as they were her favourite flower in the whole world.

Sales had been sluggish that quarter, so the first florist paused before answering, considering the ramifications of his words and the effect on his bottom line. "Ah no, we've just run out of tulips, but we're planning on getting some more in next week. Come back next Tuesday, and I'll have a beautiful bunch for you. For now, can I interest you in this gorgeous arrangement of roses?"

And so, the stranger left, a little disappointed, but distracted by her stunning bouquet of roses. And the first florist started to stock tulips.

The following Tuesday, the second florist was happily preparing tulips when a friend called from the local bakery to inform her that they had just seen a sign out the front of the first florist's shop, advertising a special on bouquets of tulips.

The second florist paused, considered her options and made her first order of roses from the local rose farm for the following Monday.

Soon, our two florists were selling both roses and tulips. They both noticed a slump in sales of their specialities and so the second florist decided to lower the price of her roses to bring in more custom. Her sales improved until the first florist got wind of it and dropped his prices.

And so began the war of the roses!

The story ends with both our florists going out of business. Why? Because they played right into the hands of greed, fear and corruption – the silent killers of business.

Let's rewind this story and do it right!

The stranger asks the first florist if they have any tulips, being that they are her favourite flower in the whole world.

The first florist pauses briefly to consider his answer, but it's a no-brainer. "No, we don't, but you're in luck because the florist down the other end of the street specialises in tulips and has some of the most beautiful blooms you will ever see!" The stranger is a little taken aback by the honesty and sincerity of the first florist and thanks them before heading down to the second florist. While purchasing her beloved tulips, the stranger mentions the kind words of the first florist and the second florist is both surprised and pleased.

Shortly after that, a person enters the second florists' shop in search of roses, and the florist has no hesitation in sending them to the first florist with a glowing recommendation.

Our florists discover that rather than compete with each other, they can complete one another. They can be the best in their field of endeavour and also help each other by letting go of the fear of missing out on a sale and looking to serve their customers and community. Their businesses flourish, and their example inspires others to do the same!

The end!

When we choose to complete others and refuse to compete, we break the cycle of pride, we choose righteousness, and we take the first steps in changing the culture of business and ultimately, our community.

WHY BUSINESSES FAIL

Here are some scary statistics. In Australia, where small businesses dominate the economic landscape, 51% fail after four years (McCrindle, 2018). The rates are almost identical in the U.S. where 50% of start-ups fail within the first five years, and by ten years it's a staggering 70% (U.S. Small Business Administration Office of Advocacy, 2018).

It seems to me that there is something fundamentally wrong with these numbers. As a Christian, I can't understand why God would call so many of us to serve our communities through business only for more than half to fail after investing money, time and energy – sacrificing on so many levels. It just doesn't fit with who I know God to be!

So, why are some businesses succeeding, but the majority fail in the short to medium term? There are a couple of fundamental reasons that we are going to explore.

1. We don't know how to do the business of doing business.

2. We lack purpose, vision and mission and have failed to consider our 'Why', 'What', 'How' and 'Who'.

WHEN WE DON'T UNDERSTAND THE BUSINESS OF DOING BUSINESS

It seems logical to me that with businesses starting up every day, there are millions of people who have a dream of some kind to be in business for themselves, and they definitely aren't planning to fail. At the same time, for every company that starts up, another is going under.

I believe that there are a bunch of reasons when it comes to high failure rates, particularly amongst the small to medium-sized enterprises (SMEs). The culture of winning at all costs, of competing rather than completing, and the lack of practical business education are a few that spring immediately to mind.

At a purely practical level, most people who go into business for themselves have expertise in a particular field or a trade. While this makes them qualified to provide a specific product or service to clients, it doesn't qualify them to run a company!

Take, for example, a plumber going into business for themselves. They've completed their apprenticeship, worked on the job for a few years and decided to become their own boss. Presumably, they've learnt the business of quoting, purchasing products and fixing people's plumbing issues – but that's not the business they now find themselves in! Instead, they now have to set up accounts, lines of credit, and ensure people are paid on time. Suddenly they are drowning in administration and caught in a cashflow crisis! The truth is that the logistics of running a business are light years away from working in your trade for someone else.

The myth is that if you have your own business – the money will flow. The reality is vastly different. Anyone contemplating going into business needs first to consider a bunch of questions! Do you understand how finances work? How about bookwork? Do you know how to employ and look after staff? And what about compliance with government policy? That last one is big because you can easily find that while you were compliant two weeks ago, this week you aren't!

Businesses end up epitomising the overused cliché "if you fail to plan, you plan to fail", and let's face it, no one wants to become a cliché.

However, of all the potential pitfalls, there is one that, if not addressed, will doom your company – even if you master the practicalities. I'm convinced that the crucial missing ingredient in many businesses, leading to a toxic culture and ultimately failure, is that leaders don't have a purpose and vision for themselves and their companies that's about more than the financial bottom line.

WHEN WE DON'T KNOW OUR 'WHY' AND 'WHAT'

Why did you go into business in the first place? Can you remember why you started on this crazy adventure? Was it to fulfil a childhood dream? Was it to be your own boss? Was it to provide for your family? While the desire to provide for ourselves and our families seems like a logical and sound reason to go into business for ourselves, it's actually not so great.

You can provide for your family in ways that are more secure and far less stressful! Starting, owning and running a business is more likely to leave you with less time to spend with your family and friends and may even threaten the very relationships you seek to care for.

If I'm honest, my reasons for starting in business were entirely selfish. I wanted nice things, I wanted to be in control, and I wanted to win. I grew up around the hospitality industry, learning the trade by watching my mother run her hugely popular hotel and then working for the opposition. By age fourteen, I was doing nicely for myself thank you very much!

I performed well academically and had a gift for math, chemistry and physics. I also had a love/hate relationship with the education system and many of my teachers. I needed a challenge, and on the whole, school failed to provide it. Instead, I made my own fun, which may have included showing my teachers up from time to time.

Some of my teachers recognised that my brain worked differently and tried to accommodate me. However, from an early age, there were those who interpreted my behaviour as troublemaking and treated me accordingly. Being a child, I reacted in kind and lived up to the label!

My parents divorced when I was 13, and as so many kids do, I blamed myself for the breakup. The divorce settlement saw me awarded to Dad, while my other siblings went to live with Mum. I interpreted that as not being wanted by my mother. Years later, I confronted Dad about it and discovered it was a practical measure implemented with the best of intentions. The family court awarded custody based on where children were living at the time of settlement, and I was the only one living with my dad at that time. The rationale, of course, was to cause as little disruption as possible to children impacted by the process of divorce. As an adult, that all makes perfect sense. As a child, with the understanding of a child, my heart and sense of worth took a battering.

Why do I share these events with you? Because we all have significant moments in our formative years that shape us and become the lens through which we perceive the world and our place in it. Our perception becomes the filter through which we view and measure success and failure. My worth and sense of self became tied to being in control and 'making it' on my own, pretty much regardless of how I hurt others along the way.

I aced my final exams and with my pick of courses I toyed with medicine but then remembered I hated the sight of blood, so followed my Dad into engineering. A year into university, I was thoroughly bored, but it was more than that. I observed my lecturers and tutors. I looked at the cars they drove, the clothes they wore and the fun they weren't having and called it quits on my university career!

I thought I had my 'why' and 'what'. I wanted nice things. I wanted to prove that I could 'make it'. I was the master of my destiny. I knew there was a god…I just thought it was me! I spent my youth waiting tables for people who enjoyed the finer things in life, and I decided that the trappings of success would be my measure. So at eighteen, when I was offered the opportunity to run a fifty-unit motel with a restaurant attached, I took it.

And here we hit the heart of the matter. In my desire to work for myself and prove that I could engineer success and carve out a dream life for myself, I fell victim to – played right into the hands of – greed, fear and corruption.

THE LIES WE BELIEVE

My vision was dependent on me winning, which necessarily meant that others must lose. I believed the lie that my worth was in the things I could accumulate, the holidays I took and the cars I drove. I was now a slave to the vision, and such visions are harsh taskmasters. When we don't know who we are, how we were made, and have an idea for the legacy we want to leave behind for future generations, we will fall for an inferior vision that will fail to satisfy our deepest heart's desires and is likely to collapse at the first hurdle.

I didn't know Jesus at this point in my life. I didn't understand that I was created in the image of the most strategic business mind in the universe. I hadn't yet felt the touch of His infinitely tender love that has since overwhelmed me, taking my broken 'why' and transforming it and me in the process. I also have to say that meeting God at the age of twenty-seven didn't instantly change my thought patterns and behaviours. I was an angry man, prone to using my words to cut people down. I thought that I was right most of the time and couldn't understand why people wouldn't just get with the programme and do what I told them!

God takes us on a journey of healing that for some is instantaneous, but for most of us, is a marathon. I'm a work in progress, but I know that my decision to say "Yes" and to keep saying "Yes" to Him has led to the wildest, crazy, most beautiful and prosperous fulfilments of vision, outstripping anything I could have imagined or hoped for.

CREATED FOR MORE

Let's revisit our original question.

"What is the ultimate reason that businesses exist?"

As I said at the start of the chapter, I believe that it's to prosper and provide for the welfare of the whole of society. I think that when businesses focus on caring for employees and communities – they flourish. I've experienced it first-hand. And when companies thrive, they steward and manage funds and resources in such a way as to prosper society.

What I'm talking about is a kingdom economy mindset. In God's kingdom, there is more than enough for all and success is measured in the way we value others, calling out the gold in people and releasing them into their identity and assignments. It's a way of living and doing business that removes limitations and allows us to tap into the creativity of the author of creation.

There is no system built by man that can accomplish what is possible with God. Capitalism, socialism, communism, Marxism (to name a few) – the collective 'isms' – have ultimately failed to deliver on their promises. None of them is inherently good or evil, better or worse. But the outworking of each – particularly when executed in isolation and to the exclusion of any other philosophy – has led to the oppression of the weakest and most vulnerable in society and obscene opulence at the opposite end of the spectrum.

> "No, O people, the Lord has told you what is good, and this is what he requires of you: to do what is right, to love mercy, and to walk humbly with your God." Micah 6:8 NLT

Business is about so much more than meeting our immediate needs or gratifying desires. You were created for more. You have been designed with passions that are unique to you and meant to benefit you, your family, community and society at large.

WHAT HAPPENS WHEN WE KNOW OUR 'WHY'!

Understanding our 'why' is critical to our vision. Our 'why' is our purpose – and may range from our reason for being on earth to the reason we are in business. Our 'why' informs our vision or our 'what', which in turn informs our mission and the goals we set.

For my wife Jane and I, our purpose, vision and mission are written in a single statement:

Our purpose is to bring heaven to earth.

Our vision is to bring hope to the nations by helping people achieve their God-given potential.

Our mission is to work with business, governmental, and other leaders around the world to help them walk in their potential and create opportunities to realise their wealth to fund kingdom growth.

This brings me to the most critical element in the success or failure of businesses, both those I've been involved with, and those I've observed over the years.

Vision.

What's your vision and is it big enough to get you through the tough times? It must be a vision that so captivates you that you can live it, articulate it, and bring others along with you. It may include elements of providing for your family, but it needs to be more. As I said earlier – if that is your primary motivation – there are more secure, less stressful ways to accomplish it.

There are a few ways to look at vision. When helping people discover their vision, be it for their lives or businesses, I get them to ask the following question; "What do I want my tombstone to say?" What do we want to be known for on this earth, and what do we want our legacy to be?

It's a big question and thinking about it can seem overwhelming. But I promise you it's worth the effort.

I'm going to have you focus on this question at the end of the chapter, but feel free to stop for a moment and let your imagination run wild.

The follow-up question is, "What needs to happen or change in my life and business for this to come to pass?"

This speaks to our legacy. What is it in the end that we want to be known for? Then we examine our lives and ask, "What needs to change to facilitate this legacy?".

Regardless of whether you have a relationship with God, this process is vital in setting your business on a trajectory for success that will benefit all it touches. The writer of Proverbs, King Solomon, known the world over for his wisdom said;

> "When there is no clear prophetic vision, people quickly wander astray. But when you follow the revelation of the word, heaven's bliss fills your soul." Proverbs 29:18 The Passion Translation (TPT)

While this advice certainly relates to having a vision for our lives and businesses and is a universal truth – it goes much further. The writer is speaking of divine revelation from God – something only possible in the context of a relationship with Him.

My experience in business is that when the vision for any given enterprise has been as the result of a revelation or idea from God, those ventures have been the most successful in every way! So much so that I find it hard to take credit for the success. My part has been to say "Yes" and to be faithful to steward the download.

Our job is to say "Yes" to Him. God doesn't need us, but He utterly delights in co-labouring with those made in His image. When it's a vision from God, it will always be about more than you and your comfort. It will benefit others and bring glory to Him. That's how you know it's from Him. It will always be so much bigger than you could dream, and it will need His divine intervention to see it come to pass.

To put it a different way; without us, there is God, and God is infinite. God could accomplish all of His plans and purposes without us but has chosen to partner with us to achieve them. Whatever we bring to the table – be it large or small – is something. And something times infinity is infinity. When we co-labour with God, we have access to an infinite mind with boundless creativity.

Conversely, if we bring nothing to the table – if we choose our 'why' over His and decide to not partner with Him, then we bring nothing to the table. And nothing times infinity is nothing. We will have a vision that may benefit our business, family, employees and community, but we will miss out on the infinite element and I, for one, don't want to miss out on an advantage like that!

THE VISION AND THE MISSION

I have a friend who epitomises what happens when people say "Yes" to God's plans. If you aren't familiar with Heidi and Rolland Baker, can I encourage you to read their story and the journey of Iris Ministries – it will challenge your ideas of what is possible! Heidi has had a dream in her heart from the heart of God for twelve years that is, quite frankly, impossible without God's intervention. And yet, she and Rolland and the team have just broken ground on Iris University in Cabo Delgado, Mozambique!

While your purpose and vision form your 'why' and 'what', the mission is your 'how' and 'who' that will bring it to fruition. As we go through the chapters – we will spend time developing our 'why', 'what', 'how' and 'who'.

When I'm speaking with business owners, I put it this way; the vision is what I'm trying to achieve, and the mission is who I'm trying to achieve it with and how we will go about it.

Your vision needs to be clearly laid out so that people know what they are signing up for. Others should be able to understand and articulate your 'why' and 'what'. Making the vision plain will mean that some don't want to be part of it. If people are only in it for the paycheque, they will most likely be the ones to leave. And that's ok! What you don't want is those that decide to stay and change the vision for their purposes. You only have to look at Moses and the Israelites wandering around in the desert for forty years to see what happens when the naysayers overrule or subvert the original vision!

One of my all-time favourite vision statements is found in the foyer of National Batteries in the U.S.

We'll bring glory to God by providing the most reliable power source in the world.

Now that's a vision statement you can get behind!

CHALLENGING THE VISION

Having said all that, allowing others to challenge the vision is a good thing! It may seem a little counter-intuitive, but any vision worth its salt will stand up to a challenge and may well benefit from the counsel of others.

"Your plans will fall apart right in front of you if you fail to get good advice. But if you first seek out multiple counsellors, you'll watch your plans succeed." Proverbs 15:22 TPT

I recommend after you have settled on your vision, that you revisit it on a yearly or even six-monthly basis to check where you are at and see where you might need to adjust to get back on track.

THE MISSION

So, you've done the hard yards and created a vision and then articulated it in a statement. Now comes the hard part (I'm joking! Not really!); the mission!

The first rule of creating the mission is that it must flow out of your vision – not the other way around. The mission must always serve the vision, and the vision should be in line with or an extension of your purpose. Your mission is the practical walking out of the vision. It has legs; it is the 'what', the 'who' and the 'how'.

If we take another look at the mission statement that Jane and I live our lives out of it states;

Our mission is to work with business, governmental, and other leaders around the world to help them walk in their potential and create opportunities to realise their wealth to fund kingdom growth.

It looks like something. We have our 'what', 'who' and 'how'; working with businesses on the ground and helping them to have both a kingdom economy and kingdom development mindset. The outworking is that they realise their wealth and have their own purpose, vision and mission that will see others blessed. It's always bigger than us.

LET YOUR YES BE YES, AND YOUR NO BE NO

One of the beauties of taking the time to develop your vision and mission statement is that it will simplify your decision making. For Jane and me, if opportunities arise that are outside our purpose, vision and mission – it's an automatic "No". It doesn't matter how good, noble or otherwise the opportunity is – it is for someone else – not us. When it's something that fits broadly in the vision – that's a reason to prayerfully consider it and see if it's something that God is asking us to do. If it sits inside the mission statement – the answer is an easy and emphatic "YES!"

REST

Strategically, there are many reasons to have our "why", "what", "who" and "how" clear for ourselves and our businesses. But for me, there is one that sits above most of them, and it didn't for the longest time. REST. Rest is not the enemy. Rest is vitally important. Our strength for the long haul is found in rest. The ability to say a clear "Yes" and "No" and to not only have times of rest but live in rest, comes when God orders our ways and plans.

If we live from our purpose, vision and mission – rest must be part of the equation. When you know what you are doing and why you are doing it – resting is not accompanied by guilt and that vague shame that many of us live with when we dare to take a break. If we don't have a clear purpose, vision and mission – we will feel compelled to jump at every opportunity that presents, and we'll end up being busy for the sake of being busy and find ourselves exhausted.

HEALING BUSINESSES

This sums up my reason for writing this book. Businesses need healing. We have lived too long in a toxic culture of greed, fear and corruption, and it has robbed us all. My heart is to set you, your business, your employees and the community around you up for success.

How can you tell if your business needs healing? What are the indicators that should alert you to areas that need to be addressed?

As we discussed earlier, we all have lenses through which we view life. Our collective understanding of the reason for business has, for the most part, been shaped by pride. The 'isms' such as capitalism, communism, Marxism, have perpetuated the problem rather than heal the inequities in wealth distribution or relieve the scourge of poverty. Our 'need' to be winners, to have it all and succeed at any cost, has led to the majority of the world's population being trapped in soul-crushing servitude.

IDENTIFIERS

Many companies have no higher purpose than to protect and increase profits. For me, this is the first identifier. If your business doesn't have a purpose, vision and mission that is beyond itself, healing is needed. It doesn't mean that everything about the company is inherently wrong – rather – that it can be better.

Beyond that, it's my firm belief that you will be able to ascertain if a business needs healing when you look at the staff. What is the turnover like in your company? How long are people staying in positions? It's true that the days of remaining in one job at a single company for thirty to forty years are long gone. Now, three to five years is the norm. If it's I.T., we might consider nine months good!

My question is "Why?" Why would people leave companies if their needs are being met? I'm not talking about projects coming to a natural end and people moving on. I'm speaking of people leaving companies for 'greener pastures' or any of the other multitude of reasons people give. I think that one of the primary identifiers that a business needs healing is when the needs of employees are not being met, resulting in a high turnover of staff, regardless of how profitable the company may be.

I believe that there needs to be a fundamental shift in the perception of business owners regarding their employees. I can hear the business owners cry, "But what about my employees?

They take my business for granted and are in it for what they can get rather than what they can contribute!"

As a business owner, I have discovered that if I change the way I view and treat my employees, they will respond in kind.

THE ROLE OF THE EMPLOYER AND EMPLOYEE

The role of the employee is to create profit for the company. No fundamental changes there. It's the employer's role that needs a whole new mindset. I believe that the role of the employer is to look after the welfare and wellbeing of their employees. Most businesses I've come across have it 180 degrees around the wrong way. Most employers focus on creating and increasing profit, while employees are trying to get their needs met, and so there is inevitably a clash. Toxic cultures are established, and people compete rather than complete.

It starts at the top. When business owners and employers are looking out for what they (and the business) can get, it breeds a culture of greed, fear and corruption that ends up with a sense of entitlement as it's outworking.

We'll talk in greater depth about how to facilitate changes in your workplace, transforming them into places of completion rather than competition and setting your business up for success. But right now, why not take some time and examine how you view your company and your employees. Take an honest look at your staff turnover and consider what precipitates team members moving on.

THE BOTTOM LINE

We've been taught to think of business as a competition, with winners and losers. I believe that there's a better way and it's about completing instead of competing. There is enough money in the world for everyone to prosper and in the kingdom economy of God, there are no losers, and there is no lack.

My experience in starting, building and running companies has shown me that when I submit to God's will for my life and am guided and directed by the Holy Spirit, He is faithful to His word. He plans to prosper us, not to harm us. His plans are to give us a hope and a future (Jeremiah 29:11).

ACTION STEPS

Get your hands on some butcher's paper or A3 sheets and write out the following questions:

1. "What do I want my tombstone to say?" or "What do I want to be known for on this earth personally, and what will my legacy be?"

2. "What do I want my company to be known for in fifty years' time beyond the provision of goods or services?"

3. "What needs to happen or change in my life and business for these to come to pass?"

This speaks to legacy. What is it in the end that I want myself and my business to be known for?

I encourage you to remove the limits of your thinking and start to dream as never before. Pray and ask God to speak to you about the vision for your life and your business. Lay it all on the table and let Him have His way. I guarantee you – it is the best way to live and do business.

Keep reading as you ponder this question over the coming hours, days and weeks.

And finally – if you haven't already, give God a go! I would be remiss if I didn't encourage you to develop a relationship with God. He is the most strategic business mind in the universe, and He loves you more than you can ever imagine. What's the worst that could happen if you connect with Him?

Jesus said that if you seek Him, if you want a relationship with Him, you will find Him. He has a plan and purpose for your life that outdoes your wildest dreams. He has a blueprint that is tailor-made and will impact the world around you for good. Your life is about more than you. Your life can leave the lives of others richer, in every way.

In chapter two, I'm going to share the story of my company, Network Neighborhood. We'll discuss the highs, the lows, the triumphs and missteps. I want my experience to help you avoid the traps and pitfalls, while giving you strategies that will change the way you think about your business.

CHAPTER TWO

The Network Neighborhood story

I founded Network Neighborhood (NN) in 1999. The lessons I learned in establishing, building and running this multi-million-dollar company were the geneses for the book you are now reading. It was as I led NN that God taught me how to run a business based on kingdom principles and with a kingdom economy mindset.

Honestly, in many ways, I find it difficult to talk about Network Neighborhood. Not because I'm afraid to share my shortcomings or the challenges we faced as a business, but because I don't think I had a lot to do with the success of the company. I said "Yes" and did what God asked of me. And then I watched Him do the most extraordinary things and still pinch myself at what happened!

It was during this time of outrageous favour that I also came face to face with my issues, fears and failures. I had to deal with toxic behaviours in every area of my life; as a husband, father, friend, business owner and leader.

Before starting Network Neighborhood, I had a diverse working background. I managed operations at leading hotel chains in Victoria before going out on my own. Jane and I successfully owned and operated award-winning restaurants and hotels, a French bakehouse, fish and chip shop, ice-cream shop and B&Bs. I wrote computer software for the insurance industry and worked in recruitment for the opening of Crown in Melbourne.

In 1998 I was asked to work in recruitment for the Telstra Union during a time of mass redundancies of its technicians. These technicians worked for Network Design and Construction (NDC) and were based in regional towns across Australia.

WHEN GOD SPEAKS

We were in the process of sorting out redundancy packages for the technicians when God spoke to me. To be more accurate, He gave me a picture and then a download. He laid out the entire vision for Network Neighborhood, from the business plan to the staff to the finances, including the projected turnover – for the next fifteen years. It was wild. It was crazy. And I had a choice.

The picture I saw, at that time, bordered on science-fiction. I saw a school, and in that school, every student carried a computing device connected to a wireless network. This idea was crazy given that in 1998, most schools had one or two computers, and the internet was still considered a novelty in most Australian homes.

I realised that the current thinking and method of delivery were never going to allow every student to connect to a network. If you have one thousand students in a school, how are they all going to log on to one system at the same time?

This kind of thing had never been done before, and there was a multitude of considerations. How do we get such a system to work? How do you secure a network like that? How do you stop students from accessing inappropriate material? How do you get a device into the hands of every student so that no one misses out?

The vision included retraining the NDC technicians as Microsoft technicians to work in local schools, building and running the networks. It was an enormous idea, but it was God's, and I had no doubt it would revolutionise the education system. I took the concept and pitched it to the union. Honestly, it was a no-brainer for me; the whole thing made perfect sense. This scheme created pathways to jobs of the future for the NDC techs while supporting local communities. Initially, the union seemed to be on board.

We approached Microsoft and COMTEC – the biggest training company in Australia at the time – and began doing roadshows for the union around the country, showing people what was possible. We started to train technicians, and across Australia, we had three hundred people trained and ready to go.

And then, just like that, the union pulled out. Why? Because they wanted to fight to keep people in jobs that didn't exist rather than create a new industry. When I think about it, I can't really blame them for doing what they had always done and what was expected by members.

I was left with my detailed vision from God that I knew would work, but not much else. Jane and I had $10,000 in the bank, and a new business partner, Norm, one of the technicians we trained who had previously run a computer business. He saw the value and potential in what we were doing and joined us at Network Neighborhood.

I felt so strongly about what God had shown me that, at the beginning of 1999, I wrote a white paper, outlining the exciting opportunities available to develop a new industry, and submitted it to the Victorian state government. I heard nothing. Later that year a tender came out from the government that was word for word (including spelling mistakes) my white paper!

We were quickly running out of resources, and so prepared a submission. In the middle of the process, there was a state election and a change of government in Victoria. The newly elected Labor government halved the amount of money on offer for the tender; another fly in the ointment of my vision from God.

THE DISTRACTION

It was at this moment I received the most enticing of opportunities. One of the large IT recruitment companies in Australia offered me the Victorian Manager's role, complete with a yearly salary of $300,000. I had a family to provide for as well as a lot of people telling me that Network Neighborhood was not going to work. I was at a crossroads. What I did was visit my pastor and mentor, Peter McHugh. I sat in Pete's office and laid out the vision of NN for Him. The only words he said were, "That sounds like God."

That was enough for me, and even though I felt completely out of control, I turned down the job offer and walked off the map of the known world!

A LESSON IN WALKING OFF THE MAP

As I said, the story of NN is only possible with God. There is just no other way that this company would have existed. It was God's idea from the get-go, and my part was to say "Yes" to Him at every step, to believe what He was telling me, and to not be distracted from the vision laid out before me.

This is life with God. It's a life that is available for everyone, not just a select few. But it comes with risk. It comes with crazy, sometimes counter-intuitive ideas and decisions that will have people around you (and sometimes you) questioning if you have heard from God.

Four weeks after turning down the job offer, we were successful in landing the tender and began the process of training technicians. I realised that if I was going to run this company, I better know what I was talking about, so I completed the Microsoft training. To my surprise, I found managing the networks and software a piece of cake!

"So, how long have you been doing this?" one of the trainers asked. "Never touched this before," I replied. "No, that's not possible!" was his response. I can only say that it was one of those gifts of God – I just knew how to do it.

And so began Network Neighborhood. There were five of us at the beginning: myself and my business partner, Norm, along with three technicians running out of a green shed. We started to pick up schools around Victoria, and by the end of our first year, we had ten technicians looking after forty schools. We worked hard, crazy hard! Being a start-up, I took on multiple roles – working as a technician, doing payroll and the books, getting home at 2am and then being back in the office at 7am to do it all again. I discovered that getting a vision from God is an invitation to hard work! We were willing to go the extra mile for schools, doing things for them that others would not, and so we grew.

As part of the tender process, we were interviewed by clusters of schools. I was personally interviewed by twelve groups, all of whom wanted to work with me. Admittedly, it was a pretty great problem to have. While considering our options, I received a call from my contact at the Department of Education who advised me to take one of the clusters over the rest. It was a good fit for us, so we said yes. This move turned out to be part of the outrageous favour of God, as the lead school in the cluster became the test site for all of the new systems and technology for the entire state. God had placed us at the forefront of the education revolution.

A TURNING POINT

By our seventh year, we were growing steadily, and I wanted to expand our operation. Norm was happy to maintain the status quo, and not interested in developing the company further. I started to talk to the Lord about buying him out and had a figure in mind.

I distinctly remember walking into a business group meeting at my church one Saturday morning and meeting the guest speaker for the morning, Peter Klomp. Peter and his wife Lynne founded the Parliamentary Prayer Network in 1993. We exchanged pleasantries, and then he spoke the words that sealed the deal.

"You've been speaking to God this morning, and there are two things. You already know what you need to do, and you know how much."

I walked back outside and called Jane, "Honey, I'm going to buy the company today, and this is what we are going to pay." "Well that's all the money in our account," was her response. "Yep, that's what God told me to do", and she agreed. I rang Norm, and five minutes later, we owned Network Neighborhood.

There is always a choice. Our choice has been to say "Yes" to God because He has proven Himself faithful. From 2007, and for the next seven years, Network Neighborhood grew at the rate of one hundred per cent, year on year.

Business was booming, and we were looking after fifty per cent of the state government-run schools in Victoria. It was at this point that the government of the day became concerned. Questions were asked like, "What if they collapse?" Considering our year-on-year growth and solid, problem-solving reputation with the Department of Education, we were quickly able to refute these assertions. Then they decided to introduce clauses like 'potential conflicts of interest' – based on us managing and leading our staff. The argument went that there was a potential conflict of interest because by managing our team well, we made more money. It was a crazy time of meetings with government lawyers with them attempting to restrict how we grew and what we could do in the sector. These are the realities of doing business, and we weren't immune to it!

Meanwhile, we had a more interesting problem. We required more and more qualified technicians to service the schools and had all but drained the pool of available resources. The solution: to approach the local TAFE (Technical and Further Education) Colleges and offer to come in and train technicians in the skills that we needed! We knew what skills were required for the market-place and so we provided comprehensive training that produced technicians job-ready for the schools. We followed this up with a mentoring programme, pairing junior technicians with senior technicians and giving them practical experience in the school environment before slotting them into the next available position.

Staff turnover was non-existent; we didn't have to advertise for new business or employees, and at this point, we had two hundred and twenty technicians with nearly $2 million a month in salaries. We decided it was time for a real office as the green shed didn't cut it anymore!

CATCHING PEOPLE DOING THINGS RIGHT!

We had a strong vision for the company that centred around creating a culture of success for our staff, clients and suppliers. We encouraged an atmosphere of excellence that included catching people doing things right. When we operate out of greed, fear and corruption – we focus on the negative – expecting people to do the wrong thing. It's like we take a perverse satisfaction in catching them out because we know it's only a matter of time. We decided to flip that culture. We chose 'righteousness' and resolved to catch people in the act of doing the right thing and celebrate it as a team!

This culture worked for most people, but not for all. We found over time that if people didn't gel with the culture, they didn't stay. It became a quick weeding out process. Our culture was about the overall team performance, and we focussed on how staff contributed to the whole.

CREATING SUCCESS FOR ALL

You may be curious about what it looks like to develop a culture of success for all. This concept became one of the hallmarks of Network Neighborhood, and I love what it did for our employees, clients and suppliers.

It comes back to the reason we are in business in the first place. As I've already shared, I believe that the ultimate goal for companies is to prosper and provide for the welfare of society as a whole. When I take care of the well-being of my employees, taking time to build relationships and caring about what matters to them, they are in turn freed to look after the business.

A big part of that is finding out what 'success' looks like for my staff. What I discovered is that the definition of success varies as widely as personality! When people are allowed to define what success looks like for them, they create a vision for their life. It's a real blessing to be a part of someone else's success!

Take the case of one of our young technicians – we'll call him 'Steve'. Steve was a handful from the start. I first met Steve when he was a student at one of the schools we supported, and he'd just been busted for hacking into the school network. A brilliant young guy, 16 years old – but headed down a wrong path. We would lock down the system, and he would get in. So, we would lock the system down again, and still, he would get in.

Eventually, I sat him down and said, "Steve, seriously, you've got two choices. You can go to jail for the stuff you're doing, or you can come and work for us." Steve was smart enough to choose us and is now one of my closest friends.

So, how do you go about creating 'success' for Steve? He is a true technician, complete with the introverted personality, and didn't really enjoy the company of others. He was also most productive between the hours of 2 and 8am. For Steve, success was being able to set his hours and work alone. So that's what we did, and Steve thrived in his new environment.

A fascinating thing happened over time with Steve. We found that as he flourished in his environment, he started to stick around and socialise and even work with others. He was given the freedom to work alone, and discovered that it fostered a desire to be around and develop relationships with his colleagues.

Others wanted to have a three-day weekend, every weekend. So we negotiated deals where they did four ten-hour days and had three days every weekend to spend with their families.

The culture of excellence and success extended to all aspects of the business. An integral part of the way we ran the company was about empowering staff to come up with solutions to the challenges that inevitably arose. I believe that we are created in the image of the Creator, and therefore, born to create. But how do we tap into the creativity of God?

> "Call to Me and I will answer you, and I will tell you great
> and mighty things, which you do not know." Jeremiah 33:3
> (NASB)

When we ask Him for creative solutions, He promises to answer us!

MAKE ME BETTER

We ran 'Make Me Better' sessions regularly. It wasn't about addressing negative behaviours – but about encouraging creativity and collaboration across the company. This is how it worked. A staff member would come to someone on leadership with an innovation or a bright idea. The response was, "Great! Now you champion the idea and clear it through the leadership team."

They would go away and prepare a fifteen-minute presentation on the concept. After the presentation, there was a thirty-minute window for people to contribute positively, making it better! Once this process was complete, the staff member had another fifteen minutes to re-present the idea with any changes or inclusions. If the concept made it through the process, we all championed the person and the project, adding resources to make it work.

The case of the dwindling pool of qualified technicians and our solution to approach TAFE Colleges offering to train technicians who could work for us came directly out of one of our 'Make Me Better' sessions. When you're intentional about creating an environment that brings the best out in people, it frees them to dream big and consider alternative solutions.

We'll take an in-depth look at the process for empowering staff in chapter five.

COMPLETING RATHER THAN COMPETING

Another hallmark of Network Neighborhood was our commitment to complete rather than compete. This philosophy permeated every part of the business, from the way we collaborated across departments, to the way we set others up for success, to our relationships with clients and suppliers.

When we compete, there are necessarily winners and losers, and our focus will be on winning. When we choose to complete, we will look for ways to lift others.

CHALLENGING THE STATUS QUO

As a business, we were kicking goals across the board. However, there were those concerned that we needed more accountability who advised us to bring higher level managers in from the outside. Honestly, it was when I bowed to the pressure and went back to the established models of doing business that things got ugly.

Things deteriorated shortly after employing several outside hires. These managers came from the corporate world and of course, had been taught to do business accordingly.

Job descriptions at Network Neighborhood were not as detailed and defined as in other businesses I've been involved with. We valued having staff who were not boxed into one area, but rather, could work collaboratively across departments for the good of the company. We paid our people well, and they received bonuses. The bonuses were given on the overall company performance, based on a formula that I developed.

As you may imagine, this flew in the face of the traditional corporate business model that depends on highly developed and specific job descriptions complete with individual KPI's (Key Performance Indicators) to determine bonuses. I chose to listen to the external advice, did what you are 'supposed' to do when your company is growing, and the new managers started making changes per their training and experience. They proceeded to rewrite job descriptions and introduce individual KPIs. Frankly, it was disastrous, and the consequences nearly killed the company.

When I realised what was happening, I tried to back out and remedy the situation, but the damage was done. The immediate effect was that it siloed staff. Where people had once worked collaboratively and across departments, they were now locked into their specific roles. Everyone was blinkered and an atmosphere of competing rather than completing infiltrated every aspect of the business.

The other outcome was that instead of leading people and managing processes and resources, the business became about managing people in their day-to-day activities. We'll go into more depth around leadership vs management in chapter three, but suffice to say, it's one way to ensure dissatisfaction amongst your staff!

I understand and agree that people need to have job descriptions and to a certain extent, KPIs. There are right and reasonable expectations that both bosses and employees should have that help to establish and maintain healthy boundaries. But I believe with all my heart that job descriptions should free people to contribute, not constrain, restrain and box them in.

It was a long, hard road back to our original culture. We had broken trust with our employees and allowed the culture of greed, fear and corruption to dictate. Not surprisingly, most of the managers we brought in left the company.

As a company, we had to redefine our vision, and as a leader, I had to humble myself before my staff and apologise, admitting that I got it wrong. There was no other way to fix this mess. I had to be accountable and transparent if I expected the staff to trust me or my words ever again. That's because, in the end, it's all about relationships. It's not about manipulating people to get them to do what I want. It's about walking and working with people in a relationship. That's how I want to be known.

For the most part, we were successful in re-establishing our culture of completing rather than competing, working together for the good of the company and our clients. However, there were aspects of the organisational change that we weren't able to undo that had a lasting impact on our culture.

THE GREAT UNDOING

When we bought Norm out and poured everything into the business in 2007, everything looked pretty amazing! And it was. And then it wasn't so fantastic for everyone around me. Underneath it all, I felt unworthy of love, rejected, and angry. Years of trying to prove myself had taken their toll on me, Jane, our families, friends and business.

I really did want the best for others and to lift them up. But in my brokenness, my identity was caught up in my perceived success or failure, and that meant I had to be in control of everything. God, in His mercy, allowed me to come face to face with my issues. In the eyes of the world, I had attained all of the material trappings of success. However, internally, I was a mess. My self-esteem was in tatters, and I took it out on those around me.

Early on in our marriage, I had an affair. I later confessed it to Jane, who graciously forgave me after working through the pain of my betrayal. We met Jesus after the affair, and while I knew that He had forgiven me, forgiving myself was another matter entirely. This, along with my unresolved self-esteem issues and the stress of the day-to-day running of NN, created the perfect storm.

I was angry, pretty much all the time. I had suicidal thoughts. I took out my stress on others by exploding with rage. As you can imagine, my relationships took a battering, and things finally came to a head.

It was Christmas Eve 2007. New contracts were flooding in, the business was succeeding, and I was running on adrenalin. Everyone around me was suffering, and Jane had borne the brunt of my inability to deal constructively with my stress.

We were due to go to her mum's for Christmas, and as we stood in the doorway of our home, she said, "Actually, I'd prefer if you didn't come to Christmas because I'm done, and we are not going to do this anymore." I moved out to stay with friends and Christmas that year was pretty wretched. Shortly after moving out, both Jane and I discovered we were suffering from adrenal fatigue. Something had to change. I had to change.

This started me on a journey of surrender to God that has transformed me, our marriage, my relationships and my style of leadership. I'll leave the details of that journey for another time. I am grateful that God loved me too much to leave me in my mess. I'm eternally grateful to Jane for showing me unconditional love in action, and I'm thankful for those who have walked with me and continue to speak into my life.

TRANSPARENCY AND ACCOUNTABILITY

While I was working through my issues with the help of God and others, I read a book that challenged, encouraged me and influenced much of what we did subsequently at NN.

Big Five for Life by John Strelecky (Strelecky, 2007, 2012), was a revelation and provided a framework and language to further develop a culture of success for me, my family, staff, clients and suppliers. I highly recommend that you read it.

The premise of the book is that we are all leaders, even if the only person we are leading is ourselves. In the book, John asks the question, "What would the greatest leader in the world look like?"

His conclusions and resulting 'Big Five for Life' so inspired me that I bought five hundred copies and gave them away to everyone I knew, including everyone at Network Neighborhood. As the leader, I wanted to take the team on the journey of discovering their 'Big Five for Life' and applying that same thinking to our company.

What I realised going into this process was that I needed to come to my staff in a spirit of openness. I had to be transparent and accountable if I was to allay fears that this was about collecting information on people that would be later used to manipulate them. This is the legacy of the culture steeped in pride.

So, I started living by example. I walked the talk and was honest about my shortcomings.

Crucially, I gave people in the company permission to speak into my life. My anger issues were no secret, and I asked them to walk alongside me and hold me accountable. When they witnessed me behaving in an unhelpful way, the question was, "Hey Hugh, do you want to go for a walk?"

We'd take a walk outside, giving me the time to cool down and the opportunity for them to speak into my world. Everyone saw this process. As a leader, my words and actions needed to align if I expected my employees to follow us into the great beyond!

SOMETHING MORE

Life is about more than our immediate satisfaction or gratification. It's about the quality of the relationships we have and the legacy we build that lifts others. Businesses have the opportunity to invest in the lives of people who would otherwise be destined to remain in poverty.

Having said that, for many years, I didn't have a social justice bone in my body! I was all about transforming the business culture from one of pride to one of righteousness, generosity and prosperous mindset, but my social conscience was limited to my community and immediate sphere of influence.

God has a way of interrupting us with His plans at the most inconvenient moments, and it was while I was working through my stuff that God spoke powerfully into Jane's world in a way that ultimately changed the trajectory of our lives.

We'll go into the full story in chapter seven, but through a series of God incidents, Jane found herself in Cambodia on a short-term mission's trip. One particular day, while visiting people who lived in the local dump, God spoke clearly to her.

"Hugh needs to come to Cambodia." Her response to God was, "Well that's good. You tell him." To which God replied, "No, I need you to do it."

To cut a long story very short, I ended up in Cambodia with my pastor and mentor, Peter McHugh. After a pretty ordinary and rather uninspiring trip, we found ourselves at the airport. That's when it happened. I saw a young boy. He wasn't doing anything in particular, not begging, just standing there, with huge eyes that looked like deep, dark holes. I said to the Lord, "Well, what do you want me to do with that?" For only the second time in my life, I heard the audible voice of God. "I want you to bring hope to the nations by helping people achieve their God-given potential."

And that was it. I was changed in a moment.

My life and my business now served a vision and mission far beyond my local community and current sphere of influence. Jane and I began investing time and money into Cambodia by supporting local businesses that rescued women from sex-trafficking and slavery – equipping them with skills to sustain themselves.

We introduced the staff at NN to our work in Cambodia and provided trips to different projects as part of bonuses. It was beautiful to see them get on board and contribute significantly. One time we ended up at a local secondary school that had been provided with new toilets including sand filters by an NGO. The problem was that they weren't connected to a water supply and were therefore unusable. This presented more of an issue that you might initially think.

When girls from the school reached puberty, they didn't have facilities to use and were too embarrassed to attend school. This resulted in them being vulnerable to being trafficked! It was crazy! So, our staff put their talents to use and provided a water tank with a gravity feed and solar pump. It cost us so little – but the implications were significant for the young women in the area.

For all of us at NN, our eyes were opened to the needs of others in the world and our collective ability to affect real and lasting change, no matter how small we may feel our part is.

THE JOURNEY CONTINUES

Network Neighborhood continued to grow and prosper. Jane and I were able to spend more and more time working on the ground in Cambodia with our businesses that employed women rescued from sex-trafficking and slavery.

The more we said "Yes" to God, the more He opened doors for Jane and me to walk through. We found ourselves removed from the day-to-day running of NN; instead, we travelled to the nations, doing the very things God promised we would do. And that was when we were approached with a buyout offer from one of Australia's largest computer retailers.

The incredible end to our role in Network Neighborhood was that as part of the vision God gave me for the business, He told me the yearly turnover. Thirteen years later, when we sold NN, there was a $13 difference from the amount I had recorded at the time of the download. God was faithful to do all He said, and He did it while working with imperfect people. All He asks is that we say "Yes" to Him. He's got everything in His hands, but He loves to create with us.

As I said at the beginning of this story, I find it difficult to take any credit for the success of Network Neighborhood. My part was to say "Yes" and remain faithful to the vision. And it wasn't me alone. The outworking of the vision depended on a group of people saying "Yes" to the possibilities and committing to action.

I once asked God why I had to sell Network Neighborhood, and His reply was, "Because I wanted all of you." I can't argue with that!

THE BOTTOM LINE

I'm not unique. I'm an ordinary person who has said "Yes" to God. There have been opportunities to walk away, and at times, it would have felt like the right thing to do. But God.

Walking with God can 'feel' counter-intuitive a lot of the time. I'm the first to admit that many of the business decisions I've made, ONLY made sense to me because He said to make them! We started Network Neighborhood with next to nothing, and we bought out my partner with all of the money in our savings because God said. I can attest that every decision made because I was faithful to a word from God has been successful. The frustrations and failures came when I took my eyes off His promises and set them on the wisdom of the world.

Looking back and reflecting on the joys, sorrows, trials and triumphs of Network Neighborhood, I'm beyond thankful for the opportunity to say "Yes" to God's plans. I'm humbled that we got to work with the greatest mind in the universe to help transform the education system in Victoria. I'm grateful for all of those who said "Yes" and walked off the map with me.

ACTION STEPS

We often get so busy doing business that we don't take time to reflect on the journey so far and dream for the future. Right now, take some time to sit and think about where you have come from, where you are going and what you want for yourself, business, staff and clients.

What does it look like for you to focus on catching people in the act of doing things right? It could be celebrating the person who quietly fills the paper tray for the photocopier. Or that co-worker who always has a smile and an encouraging word for others. If we are going to transform our workplaces, we need to shift our gaze from the negative to the positive. And it's fun! Can you imagine every person in your workplace looking for the best in others and appreciating the efforts of those they spend a third of their lives with?

Below are some questions to help you process;

1. What risks have you taken in your business? What has worked? What hasn't? Why?

2. What are your dreams for your business?

3. If you have a relationship with God, what are His dreams for your business?

4. What does it look like for you to say "Yes" to God in your business?

5. What are your hopes and dreams for your staff and/or co-workers?

6. What kind of culture would you like to champion in your workplace?

7. How have you contributed to the culture of your workplace; positively and negatively?

8. What does it look like for you to 'catch' people in the act of doing things right?

9. Take a moment to consider those you can celebrate in the coming weeks.

In chapter three, we are going to get back to the basics of leadership and discover what it looks like to embrace vulnerability, transparency and accountability. It's time to get real about owning our stuff!

CHAPTER THREE

Identity, self-awareness and leadership

BACK TO BASICS

In the end, life is about relationships. It's about a connection with others. For me, it's about my connection with God and people made in His image. Everything comes back to this fundamental truth. I want the lives of others to be better because I am on the planet. I desire every part of my life to display the goodness and kindness of God. Why? Because God has been so good to me, and His love moves me to love others.

I'm acutely aware that to live a life that benefits others, I must know who I am and whose I am. If I'm secure in my identity and embrace my need to be in a relationship with others, I can lead in a way that lifts people and sets them up for success. If I don't have these truths as my foundation, the way I do life, relate to others and run my business will emanate from a distorted perspective.

I believe that this is why the toxic culture of greed, fear and corruption thrives in business, finding expression in the way we compete rather than complete. We have leaders who don't know who they are and so are unable and often unwilling to help others become all that they can.

Some wise person said that we can only give away what we've received. If I can accept and embrace the truth that I am unique and loved by the master designer, I am more likely to be able to call the gold out in others – particularly in those who work for me. We are each called to be ourselves, the people we were designed to be, and that the world needs us to be.

I wish I could say that I discovered these truths at a young age and that they've been the hallmark of my thirty-plus years in business, but that would be a lie. I could tell you that when Jane and I met Jesus, I had an epiphany about how I should treat people and was never the same again, but that wouldn't be true either.

The fact is that I have been a work in progress ever since accepting Jesus into my life and while I'm a quick study in many areas of life, it's taken many years and a lot of damaged relationships for me to change.

In this chapter, we are going to look at what it means to lead and why knowing yourself and owning your stuff matters. We're also going to explore the difference between leadership and management and set you on a course to lead your business authentically with vulnerability and transparency.

So, let's do this and set our employees and businesses free to be all that they were meant to be!

IDENTITY AND SELF-AWARENESS MATTER

When I was a teenager, I loved Footy. Now I'm an Aussie from Victoria, so when I say 'Footy', I'm not talking about the 'beautiful game' of soccer, I'm talking about the 'glorious game' of AFL Football! I was mad about it. I wasn't a natural, and I was never going to be an AFL star, but I loved to play and was committed.

It was entirely at odds with the rest of my family who were mad keen sailors. In my defence, I gave it a go, but I hated it! AFL was my thing and a stabilising influence in my life during a pretty turbulent emotional time. My parents had recently divorced, and I blamed myself for their breakup. My four siblings were awarded to Mum while I lived with Dad. All of this fed the lie I believed; that I wasn't loved and that I was fundamentally unworthy of love.

Now, I'm not a great sportsman, and my hand-eye coordination is pretty ordinary, but I loved AFL, and I worked harder than just about anyone. I would run the 5kms from home to the footy oval, train, and then run home. I trained with the seniors and the juniors but was only ever picked as the reserve, often missing out on a game.

Mum was busy running the local hotel and wasn't able to make it to my games. Dad was so busy with work that he didn't realise I was even interested in footy, let alone played. I felt invisible to my family. Then along came Mrs Taylor, a parent of one of the other boys. She watched me train, saw my dedication, and convinced the coach to give me a go. The following year I played every game and did very well in the voting for Best and Fairest on field. It wasn't because I'd transformed into a supreme athlete but because I worked hard, was a team player, and had someone who believed in me.

I share this with you for a couple of reasons. The first is that I grew up believing the lie that I was unworthy of love. I tried to prove myself by 'succeeding' in business and life. I bought into the culture of greed, fear and corruption, and I didn't own my stuff, causing a great deal of pain to me, my family and those in my employ.

How did this play out in business? Well, I thought that my way was the only way. After all, if I'm right all the time – then maybe I'm worthy of love. We've all seen or had bosses who have to be right, with staff in a constant state of stress, second-guessing every decision and fearful of making mistakes.

As leaders in business, we must first own our stuff. If we can let go of our ego and give our pride a rest, we permit others to deal with their stuff! If we expect others to grow and change – we have to be willing to go there ourselves.

We all have experiences in our past that colour the way we see and operate in the present. Great leaders aren't those without issues or even those who have worked through them. Great leaders own that they have stuff and do something about it!

Your employees are looking for authenticity. We can't just overlay our lives with a new structure and expect to fake it till we make it. If we want to affect transformation in our businesses, we must be willing to admit that we don't have all the answers and are not always right. We must learn to be vulnerable and transparent if we are going to ask our employees to trust us and buy into the vision and mission of the business.

It begins at the top. It starts with me owning my stuff, owning my toxic behaviours and the at times unrealistic expectations I have had of those around me. If you want to create a culture of honour, it begins with vulnerability, transparency and accountability for your actions. It's easy to end up paying lip service to these weighty matters. I don't list them lightly, and I understand the cold sweat they may elicit. Being vulnerable is a scary concept for most people, but for leaders, it can be downright terrifying!

OWNING YOUR STUFF

Owning your stuff is an essential step in flipping a prideful culture. I've said it a few times already, but it's a vital ingredient. If we as leaders don't own our stuff, we can't complain when others follow our example. Trust me; I know what I'm talking about. I spent years not owning my stuff, lost in my insecurities and trying to prove myself to the universe!

Jane and I met Jesus in 1992. We had recently arrived back on the mainland of Australia after spending two years in Tasmania with my mum, step-dad and our young daughter. We transformed the local red-brick pub in the town of Woodbridge into an award-winning establishment, voted 'Australia's Most Popular Restaurant' in 1991.

We worked hard to build relationships with local suppliers, featured local produce in our menu, and employed people from the community. We recommended other local restaurants and often had the owners come in for a meal. There was much to be proud of, and yet, my feelings of unworthiness were out of control. To compensate, I controlled and micro-managed everything around me.

There was no balance. I worked incessantly and to be honest, it was convenient. It meant that I didn't have to build personal relationships, and it kept me at arm's length from those I loved.

Work is a great way to hide – for a while. However, you can't escape yourself, and in the end, Jane had enough of the loneliness and isolation and moved back to Melbourne, heavily pregnant with our second daughter.

I stayed on to work at the pub until Jane found a house, but my inner turmoil had repercussions beyond business, and I made the monumentally stupid decision to have an affair.

I share this story because I did not own my stuff, and so finally, my stuff owned me! It has always been this way. I'm certainly not saying it will inevitably lead to moral compromise, but the state of our heart will invariably find its expression in our actions.

> Watch over your heart with all diligence,
> For from it flow the springs of life.
> Proverbs 4:23 (NASB)

There is a choice for you to make as a leader, and if you think you are off the hook as an employee, consider the words of John Strelecky, author of *The Big Five for Life*,

> *"We are all leaders, even if we are only leading ourselves"*
> (Strelecky, 2007, 2012)

We can deal with the reality of our humanity in one of two ways;

1. We can be prideful and pretend that we are always right. Let me save you some time, that's the wrong choice. The fruit of that particular tree is poisonous.

2. We can be humble and change everything that's not working. It's the best way, but it's not easy. Learning to walk in humility is hard because it involves laying everything down and being vulnerable.

When we choose to walk in the way of humility, it means that we choose words that speak life over those that produce death. For every prideful word, there's another that's humble. We must then follow our words up with actions. We must be able to lift those around us, releasing them to be all that they can.

It's a journey. In my opinion, good strong leaders are that for a reason. They work to bring out the best in those around them, and they do it for the right reasons. If we are doing it for self-gain – it will ultimately fail. If we are genuinely seeking to promote others – it will work.

LEADERSHIP VS MANAGEMENT

As an employer and a leader, my role is to help others in my business discover who they are and what they were designed to do. That means I ensure that they have the training, the tools and the support they need so that they can bring their all to the business, knowing that I am for them.

It may sound like a utopian fantasy that lets people do whatever they want; but in fact, transparency and accountability are the glue that holds people together. When people feel supported and valued, robust discussions and disagreements happen regularly. The difference is that fear is removed from the equation. We are human beings and conflict will inevitably occur. As a leader, I must commit to working through conflict in a constructive manner, allowing others to have a voice and letting them change my mind if it's warranted.

I certainly wasn't perfect at this, and I knew it! I asked others in the company to help me by speaking into my life and holding me to account. Honestly, it's hard to let others pull you up as a leader. Pride is a powerful motivator. The pervading culture of greed, fear and corruption thrives because it feeds the ego, particularly for those at the top. At the same time, pride breeds resentment in those lower down the pecking order.

Nobody is perfect. Leaders are not perfect. I know that for the first few years in Network Neighborhood, I thought I was the ideal leader because the business was thriving. It was only after we bought out my partner that I came face to face with my glaring imperfections.

The problem with leaders believing their spin is that their expectations of others get entirely out of whack. I thought that the success of the business was due to my decisions and my ability. I had to take a step back and learn to make it about other people. There were two reasons for this – for their good and the good of the company.

When I finally got my head around this truth – we were able to celebrate the incredible success together, as a group. I had to learn that it wasn't all about me, and my employees needed to have ownership of the business as well. It's not about abdicating responsibility as a leader. There were still days when I needed to be the one making the decisions. There were the executive decision moments, where I said, "We are going this way." Honestly, there were days when I upset people who disagreed with a particular decision I was making, but that is part of being the owner and leader of a business. I respected their opinion, but I needed to be true to the vision of the company. The difference is that those moments are not the norm. Your staff will be more likely to respect and accept your captain's calls when they are the exception rather than the rule.

Now, back to my AFL playing days. The second reason I shared that story is to remind us of the power we have to make a positive difference in the lives of others. Mrs Taylor chose to go into bat for me and showed what it was to have someone believe in me. Her actions had a profound and lasting impact on my life. She did what a great leader does – see the gold in others and call it out. Contrast that with the coach of the team, who was in a management role. He focussed on allocating resources and going for the win, but not necessarily looking to empower individual players.

Real leadership casts a vision for others to grab hold of and own. Great leaders understand that their role is to help others soar to greater heights than they have reached. Greatness in others isn't a threat. Strong leaders take the time to discover, encourage and empower people because they are secure in their identity and understand they cannot bring the vision to pass without others. Jesus is my role model in this, as in all things.

> "I tell you this timeless truth: The person who follows me in
> faith, believing in me, will do the same mighty miracles that
> I do – even greater miracles than these because I go to be with
> my Father! For I will do whatever you ask me to do when
> you ask me in my name. And that is how the Son will show
> what the Father is really like and bring glory to him. Ask me
> anything in my name, and I will do it for you!" John 14:12-14
> The Passion Translation (TPT)

Jesus set His disciples and all who follow Him up for success! He wasn't afraid of others. He celebrated, championed, equipped, empowered and released us to do more than He ever did on the earth. Crucially, all of this happened and continues to happen today in the context of love and relationship. We cannot escape it, no matter how much we may want to. Unless we do everything from a basis of love – it will eventually fall away. We cannot manipulate our way through life, and if we seek to manage those around us, it will ultimately come home to roost.

Let's contrast relational leadership with the concept of management, which is an entirely different beast. Leadership is about teaching, training, equipping, empowering and releasing. Management, on the other hand, is about education, training (sometimes), but not necessarily about equipping, and hardly ever about empowering people. The problem with management is that it tends to compartmentalise and restrict employees, confining them to narrow, highly specified parameters within which they must operate. When you manage people, they report to you, and you handle them and the task. You are over the top of them, directing and controlling. It verges on a master/slave scenario where people are not empowered or released to run with a vision.

I think we've created a society full of businesses that are being over managed and under led. We've built layers of management in, and it's not that they are entirely unnecessary, but that they are designed to value task over people.

So, what does it look like to lead companies rather than manage them? Let me walk you through the steps we took at Network Neighborhood to shift the culture from one of management to leadership that trained, equipped, empowered and released people to discover and walk in their success while growing the business one hundred per cent year on year for seven years.

What does that look like practically? Firstly, we took the time to get to know our staff. We stopped making assumptions, (which, let's face it are usually negative) about each other's motives and sought to connect with and understand one another. I helped the process by introducing the team to the book *Big Five for Life*. I bought everyone a copy of the book, and we helped staff members discover their own 'why', 'what', 'how' and 'who'. We then worked on success plans for the business and each member of the team. We'll go into detail about what this looked like in chapter four.

Yes, it took time. There is no getting around the investment of time and energy on my part and that of the leadership team. I can say, without hesitation, it was worth it. It demonstrated to the staff that I was serious about looking after them and that they were valued as individuals, over and above what they could do for my business. Of course, some got on board faster than others. It takes time to develop trust, and the culture of greed, fear and corruption sets up mistrust of authority. For some of my staff, they feared that if I found out their vision for success, I would use that knowledge to manipulate and control. I found that the best way to allay fears was to follow up my words with action. I shared my vision for success with the whole team. After all, I couldn't expect them to share with me if I was not willing to be open and vulnerable.

Leaders let their actions speak louder or at least at the same volume as their words. At Network Neighborhood, success plans were the tangible evidence that I valued my employees as unique individuals. Success plans were such a hit that we began looking for ways to create them for our clients and suppliers.

Vitally, the process of creating success plans for the staff helped to develop relationships across the team. It helped me to understand the core values and motivations of the people I worked with every day.

I didn't always get it right. I was still working through my stuff. There were times that I fell back into old habits and had to, once again, make myself vulnerable and accountable. I know I've already said this, but it's important and bears repeating. As a leader, one of the most significant characteristics I can cultivate in my life is humility.

Rick Warren in his book, *A Purpose Driven Life*, put it so well,

"Humility is not thinking less of yourself; it's thinking of yourself less" (Warren, 2002)

I can't remember how I came across it, but one day I found a list with fifty attributes of humility on one side and fifty prideful traits on the other. I was a bit horrified to discover, as I worked my way through the sheet, that I had far more on the pride side of the list. Up to that point, I thought I was doing all right. I realised that I needed to learn what humility means.

LEADING, GOD'S WAY

But the fruit produced by the Holy Spirit within you is divine love in all its varied expressions: joy that overflows, peace that subdues, patience that endures, kindness in action, a life full of virtue, faith that prevails, gentleness of heart, and strength of spirit. Never set the law above these qualities, for they are meant to be limitless. Galatians 5:22-23 The Passion Translation (TPT)

There are some traps that leaders fall into (and I did) when we are in the process of transforming our business culture into one that empowers and releases our teams. In our zeal to build a culture that values the contributions of others and looks for ways to promote, we can forget that we too are in the process of transformation. If we aren't careful, our leadership style can end up resembling Jekyll and Hyde, confusing everybody we are trying to lead in the process!

One of my earliest mistakes was to remove myself from important decision making too soon. I was so keen to empower and release that I delegated when I still needed to be at least a guiding presence and, in some instances, the decision maker. When you delegate and then swoop in because of a 'wrong' decision, it sabotages the confidence you are trying to instil in people.

Again, we find ourselves back at relationships; needing to be open and accountable, talking these situations through with our staff. As leaders, we walk a fine line. Nobody wants a doormat for a boss, but neither do they want one who regularly criticises and controls. Most of us tend to swing between the two extremes, attempting to find a balance somewhere along the way. We need to keep the dialogue open with our teams as we transition the culture – or risk littering the lunchrooms and hallways of our businesses with figurative dead bodies!

Of course, Jesus took it a step further. He declared that there was an even higher way.

"For the greatest love of all is a love that sacrifices all. And this great love is demonstrated when a person sacrifices his life for his friends." John 15:13 The Passion Translation (TPT)

For me, real leadership is the way that Jesus lived. His is the ultimate example. He didn't ask His disciples to do anything He wasn't willing to do Himself. As a leader and employer, my role is to look after the wellbeing and welfare of my staff so that they are free to bring their best to my company and become all that they are meant to be.

WISDOM IN THE COUNSEL OF MANY TRUSTED ADVISORS

> Your plans will fall apart right in front of you if you fail to get good advice.
>
> But if you first seek out multiple counsellors, you'll watch your plans succeed. Proverbs 15: 22 The Passion Translation (TPT)

A mistake I made early on in the running of Network Neighborhood was that I didn't bring in enough of the right trusted people. I told myself that because we were successful, we could go it alone, but that was a half-truth. The whole truth was that I was still operating out of brokenness on many levels, and my pride was informing much of my decision making.

The problem with not gathering the right people around you from the start is that eventually, you will need people and you will be more likely to choose the wrong ones. My inability to let people in to speak into my business in the early days set the scene for bringing in managers who did not understand our 'why', 'what', 'how' and 'who'. They knew how to manage a business based on an economic bottom line and a model of competing rather than completing. That meant they were never going to be a fit for NN. I didn't stop for long enough to consider the ramifications of bringing them in, partly because I was so busy that I lost sight of the bigger picture. I compromised my vision of cultural transformation and settled for an inferior vision for the sake of expediency.

Do you have trusted people, both inside and outside your business, who understand your purpose, vision and mission? Do they have permission to speak into your world and your business?

If not, why? It's time to consider what, if anything, has stopped you from seeking the wise counsel of others.

As I shared in the last chapter, it was a long road back from the mistakes we made, and some aspects of the culture never recovered. I strongly urge you to think and pray about whom you need to connect with to see your business move from good to better; better to best.

COMMUNICATION

"The single biggest problem in communication is the illusion that it has taken place." (Whyte, 1950)

I suspect that communication, good or bad, doesn't come naturally to the vast majority of human beings. I believe it requires training and a commitment to learning on our part. Moreover, like everything else in life, it comes down to relationships. Communication implies and requires dialogue, give and take. If we aren't building relationships – we can't expect to engage in meaningful interaction. The way we communicate is also vital in our face-to-face dealings with one another. For a long time, my anger issues shut people down. That meant not only was there no meaningful dialogue, but they also tuned me out to protect their hearts.

Part of my job as a leader is to bring people on the journey by creating a culture of honest, respectful dialogue. It's much easier to do when you have a clearly articulated vision that people are invited to contribute to and own. We need to resist the urge to impose our vision and mission without asking others to join the conversation about our collective and individual 'why', 'what', 'who' and 'how'. If all we do is implement a vision and mission without addressing the foundational issues of greed, fear and corruption – we will end up with window dressing that will fade and fall away when exposed to the inevitable pressures of doing business.

Clear communication helps to establish an atmosphere of safety and trust. In that space, there is a grace for people to be themselves, to own their stuff and contribute positively in the workplace. Communication is more than the words we speak. It's the way we talk and the body language that accompanies it. The ability to communicate effectively, up, down, across and sideways is also the ability to influence. If you haven't learnt the art of communication, you haven't mastered the art of influence.

Jesus was a master of communication and an unsurpassed influencer. If you read any of the gospels, He spent most of His time telling stories and asking questions. Jesus rarely answered questions directly. Instead, He engaged people in conversation and got them to think – deeply. He valued people, and so He appreciated their thoughts. We tend to believe we have communicated with others when we tell them what to do, rather than engaging in a meaningful discussion that unlocks and unleashes creativity and ultimately strengthens relationships.

I realised that I had to model this sort of communication at Network Neighborhood, particularly given my track record of rage-fuelled outbursts. The first thing I did was look for the gold in others rather than assuming the worst of everybody around me. When immersed in the culture of greed, fear and corruption, we are more likely to blame and shame rather than show grace and compassion. Owning my stuff made me far more aware of the fact that other people are, by and large, trying to do the right thing while dealing with their stuff! I learned to soften my approach and to take the time to find out what was going on with others rather than charging in with veiled accusations or directions.

Our Creator has endowed us with good brains, big hearts, and the ability to learn the art of communication; engaging with and valuing others. It's your choice, but I believe it's vital in flipping the culture of your business, or for that matter, family, church, club, or friendship group.

LEADERSHIP THAT LIFTS

I've said it before, and I'll repeat it, leaders are not perfect. Let's say it together, "Leaders are not perfect". You will doubtless have picked up that while the team and I got many things right at NN, I also got a fair few things wrong. I found out the hard way what happens when leaders fail to engage with their team. Spoiler alert: it results in reasonably spectacular chaos!

One stand out moment of confusion was the night I decided to rearrange the office layout. While it may seem a relatively trivial matter, I discovered that the devil is in the detail! Things were getting physically tight in our limited office space, and I'd been mulling over how to alleviate the problem. I figured out the best way to make use of the area, which involved moving furniture and people. That's all fine and dandy, but I failed to do one crucial thing. I forgot to bring others in on my vision for change, particularly those it would directly affect. You may carry an incredible vision for your company, but if you are the only one who owns it, the results will most likely be the opposite of what you intend!

I mapped out in my mind the best course of action. I knew where I wanted people to sit, what was the most functional layout possible given the available space, and how it would improve the workflow of the office. What I didn't take into account was how others would feel about being moved without consultation or warning. My triumph quickly became my mess as chaos erupted the next morning.

Here's what I learned in my mess;

1. While I placed no value on where I was positioned physically in the office, for others, it mattered enormously. In summarily moving them, I inadvertently devalued what mattered to them.

2. People are not generally against change. Most people accept and embrace change when presented respectfully, and the process is open. What they don't like is having change foisted upon them with no ability to have input.

3. Being a leader is about bringing people on a journey. It's about being collaborative, not dictating from on high and expecting people to get on board without explanation.

In hindsight, I should have called a meeting, presented the problem and asked for ideas and submissions. The process might have taken a couple of extra days, but consultation and collaboration would have valued my staff, their opinions and ultimately, their contribution to the company. In keeping my thoughts to myself and charging ahead, I also missed opportunities to strengthen relationships that I had cultivated intentionally.

HEALTHY BOUNDARIES

I want to touch briefly on setting healthy boundaries, particularly as you own and deal with your stuff and allow space for others to do the same. Communication is critical in establishing safety and trust while everyone deals with their stuff. Healthy boundaries are possible when the expectations are clear, mutually agreed upon, and all understand processes for addressing issues.

It's about managing processes and leading people in transition. Remember that in the process of change, people will sometimes fall back into old behaviours. When I was addressing my anger issues, I tried hard, but there were times when I'd fail. Old habits die hard, particularly ones generated over the decades. Jane had to exercise much grace while I learned a better way. I don't mean she tolerated bad behaviour on my part, but instead, she saw it now as the exception rather than the rule and loved me through it while keeping me accountable for my actions.

It's easy to believe that people aren't changing when we see the same old behaviour. As leaders we need to engage our teams with clear communication that helps them transition rather than shaming them into good behaviour that sabotages real and lasting change.

THE BOTTOM LINE

If we want to transform our organisational culture from greed, fear and corruption to caring, sharing and prosperity for all, we must lead the way. We must be the forerunners of all that we desire to see in our businesses, and we have to own our stuff before we can expect anybody else to follow suit. That's how we ensure our vision and mission don't become empty rhetoric. We must value people over profit, and that includes learning to love and accept ourselves. My breakthrough came when I admitted that I felt unworthy of love and needed to experience the love of God and people.

Pivotal in my process was finding a mentor who loved me enough to give me honest feedback on my behaviour and gently suggest areas that needed to change. It takes humility to admit that we have blind spots, that we have issues, that we are human and that we get it wrong sometimes. If we can model what it looks like to own our stuff, we will set ourselves, our staff and our businesses up for outrageous favour.

If pride comes before a fall, then humility comes before the soar!

There's very little room for ego when you decide to flip a culture. If we genuinely want to see a generous culture emerge, one that's rooted and grounded in authentic relationships, humility is one of the essential ingredients.

For those blooded in a toxic culture, where pride equals strength and leadership is above questioning, it's a tough transition. It was hard for me. Even as the business grew, I found myself undone and on my knees before God. I had to surrender every part of my life to Him, so don't be surprised if you find your life seemingly falling apart as you take this journey.

As Graham Cooke puts it,

"When God's putting the finger on the part of your life that's not working, He's pointing to your next miracle." (Cooke, 2017)

It's an invitation to an upgrade. If I had continued to live feeling unworthy of love and trying to prove myself – I would have maintained my rage and most likely lost my family and business.

Each of us is responsible for stewarding the gift God has given us. Our businesses are about more than us – they have the God-given potential to benefit the whole of society. If you haven't already, ask God to give you His perspective on your business.

You may be surprised at His answer, and if you don't know Him personally yet, I can only encourage you to give Him a go. You won't be disappointed!

ACTION STEPS

It's time to think about where you are right now. I've included some questions to help you process your thoughts and I encourage you to take some time to consider and record your answers.

1. Have you owned your stuff?

2. What aspects of your 'stuff' own you?

3. What can you do this week to own more of your stuff?

4. Do you have trusted advisors who understand the 'why', 'what', 'who' and 'how' of your business?

5. Are there any blind spots you need to address?

6. Do you have a mentor?

7. Take some time to work your way through the 'Pride vs Humility' table on the following pages. There is no judgment attached to this exercise – it's a tool to help you identify the areas that require tweaking. Again, if we are asking others to own their stuff – we need to be honest and humble enough to call out the areas we need to work on.

	Proud people	Humble people
1	Focus on the failures of others	Are overwhelmed with a sense of their own spiritual need
2	Have a critical, fault-finding spirit; look at everyone else's faults with a microscope but their own with a telescope	Are compassionate, can forgive much because they know how much they have been forgiven
3	Are self-righteous; look down on others	Esteem all others better than themselves
4	Have an independent, self-sufficient spirit	Have a dependent spirit; recognise their need for others
5	Have to prove their are right	Are not argumentative
6	Claim rights; have a demanding spirit	Yield their rights; have a meek spirit
7	Are self-protective of their time, their rights, and their reputation	Are self-denying
8	Desire to be served	Are motivated to serve others
9	Desire to make a name for themselves	Are motivated to be faithful and to make others a success
10	Desire self-advancement	Desire to promote others
11	Have a drive to be recognised and appreciated	Have a sense of their own unworthiness; are thrilled that God would use them at all
12	Are wounded when others are promoted, and they are overlooked	Are eager for others to get credit and rejoice when others are lifted up
13	Have subconscious feeling that says, "This organisation is privileged to have me and my gifts"; think of what they can do for God	Have a heart attitude that says, "I don't deserve to have any part in this work"; know that they have nothing to offer God except what He enables them to do

	Proud people	Humble people
14	Feel confident in how much they know	Are humbled by how very much they have to learn
15	Are self-conscious	Are not concerned with self at all
16	Keep others are arms' length	Are willing to risk getting close to others and to take risks of loving intimately
17	Are quick to blame others	Accept personal responsibility and can see where they are wrong in a situation
18	Are unapproachable or defensive when criticised	Receive criticism with a humble, open spirit
19	Are overly concerned with what others think; work to protect their own image and reputation	Are concerned with being real; what matters to them is not what others think but what God knows; are willing to risk their own reputation
20	Find it difficult to share their spiritual needs with others	Are willing to be open and transparent with others as God directs
21	Want to be sure that no one finds out when they have sinned; their instinct is to cover up	Once broken, don't care who knows or finds out; are willing to risk their own reputation
22	Have a hard time saying, "I was wrong; will you please forgive me?"	Are quick to admit failure and to see forgiveness when necessary
23	Tend to deal in generalities when confessing sin	Are able to acknowledge specifics when confessing their sin
24	Are concerned about the consequences of their sin	Are grieved over the cause, the root of their sin

	Proud people	Humble people
25	Are remorseful over their sin, sorry that they got found out or caught	Are truly repentant over their sin; forsake their sin
26	Wait for the other to come and ask forgiveness when there is a misunderstanding or conflict in a relationship	Take the initiative to be reconciled when there is a misunderstanding or conflict in the relationship, no matter how wrong the other may have been
27	Compare themselves with others and feel worthy of honour	Compare themselves to the holiness of God and feel a desperate need for His mercy
28	Are blind to their true heart condition	Walk in the light
29	Don't think they have anything to repent of	Realise they have need of continual heart attitude of repentance
30	Don't think they need revival but are sure that everyone else does	Continually sense their need for a fresh encounter with God and for a fresh filling of His Holy Spirit

(DeMoss and Grissom, 2004. Used with permission.)

In chapter four, we are going to continue to challenge conventional paradigms by looking at our definitions of success and failure, expectation and expectancy, and so much more. Are you ready? Let's do it.

CHAPTER FOUR

Failure and success

FLIPPING THE CULTURE

What springs to mind when you picture 'success'? Stop for a moment and think about what success looks like for you and what it looks like for your business. Now consider the word 'failure'. What comes immediately to mind? Have you noticed that failure is more of an objective measure and more easily identified, while success is subjective and can differ wildly from person to person?

When we don't own our stuff, are not secure in our identity and don't know our 'why', 'what' 'who' and 'how', our measure of success will be at the mercy of the culture of greed, fear and corruption. We are more likely to allow the 'success' or 'failure' of our business to be defined by competing rather than completing and an 'I must win; therefore, you must lose' mentality. The good news is that we have the opportunity to transform our business culture by challenging the 'winners and losers' narrative and creating one that values people above profit. Why? Because business is about people, and it's time that we look beyond ourselves to the welfare of others and the benefit of our communities.

RISK VS REWARD

The catch cry of so many in business is 'risk versus reward' or 'return on investment' (ROI). While assessing the ROI on an investment or business opportunity is part of due diligence, how you measure it makes all the difference. Economics is the study of the allocation of scarce resources. It's a poverty mentality, and when we view opportunities through the eyes of this economic ideology, we are doomed to operate from lack and with a limited pie mentality. It's a poverty mentality that breeds more poverty for the majority of the world's population. It's time to challenge the status quo and question our definitions of 'success' and 'failure', 'risk and reward'. It's the radical nature of moving from fear to favour and requires a deliberate change of direction on our part.

In this chapter, we're going to challenge the status quo by asking a bunch of questions like; how do we define success and failure in our lives and our business? What do we expect of our employees and what should they expect of us? How do we lead with authenticity, releasing others to discover their success? How can we communicate effectively with our teams and ensure they have a voice in the process?

Finally, we're going to get down to the practical steps involved in creating success plans for you, your business and your team. I can't wait to share the actions that you can take now to flip the culture in your organisation and set your business free!

Let's start by revisiting the role of the employer and the employee. The part of the employee is to create profit for the company. The role of an employer is to look after the welfare and wellbeing of their employees.

As I said in chapter one, it starts at the top. When business owners and employers only care about what they can get out of their employees, it breeds a culture with pride at its core. The outworking is usually the opposite of what leaders desire. Instead of motivated employees working for the good of the company, you end up with a bunch of people who are also looking out for themselves (go figure!). It usually manifests as an exaggerated sense of entitlement that perpetuates the culture of greed, fear and corruption. Everybody feels like they are trapped in the rat race with retirement the only escape.

We must be the circuit breaker! We need to lead the way and model what we want to see in our communities. We have one life to live, and it has to be about more than going through the motions or climbing over others to get our piece of the pie.

SUCCESS IS ABOUT MORE THAN ME

For most of my life, I thought that if everyone just did things my way, and as I directed, they would be successful. This attitude permeated every aspect of my life. Even after meeting Jesus at twenty-seven, I still operated out of my brokenness, perceiving the world through the lens of unworthiness and rejection.

For the longest time, I measured my success by my financial and business accomplishments, with the material trappings as the evidence of that success. I didn't understand that my perception of success was not the one carried by others. I certainly didn't get that for Jane, her measure of success involved me valuing our relationship and having time at home with her and the kids.

I thought I knew what I wanted from life. I thought I knew what was important. That was until I did the 'Tombstone Test' (see 'Action Steps' in chapter one), and asked myself, "What do

I want to be known for on this earth and what do I want my legacy to be?" I came to the crushing realisation that my life didn't add up. What I wanted to be known for did not match how I was known.

If we are going to take our businesses from pride to righteousness, we need to examine what success and failure look like for us, our families, businesses and employees. We must address, and at times expose the expectations we have of others and whether or not they are realistic and reasonable. We need to get real and have honest conversations about the expectations of our employees to make sure we're all on the same page moving forward.

When we take the time to really listen and communicate respectfully, honouring each other even as we challenge and allow others to challenge our thinking, we build relationships. In the end, that's what matters. In the end, all we have is relationships, and they will either be healthy and robust or end up with some degree of toxicity.

The bottom line is that we can have the best will in the world along with an incredible vision and mission, but if we fail to communicate effectively with our staff, we will fail. Period!

EXPECTATIONS VERSUS EXPECTANCY

Have you ever thought about the difference between expectancy and expectations? 'Expectation versus Expectancy' sounds cliché, and it would be easy to gloss over the distinction, but I want us to stop and consider their respective meanings.

Expectancy has hope at its core. There's an anticipation that something good will happen. For me, expectancy lives in the same space as the culture of generosity, completing others, and caring, sharing and prosperity for all. Expectancy gives room to breathe. It doesn't claim to have all the answers but invites others to the table to contribute strategies and solutions in the pursuit of our collective 'why'.

Expectation, on the other hand, is; "a strong belief that something will happen or be the case." (dictionary.com, 2018)

With expectation, there is a certainty as to the outcome. The confidence is in the mind of the one with the expectation, and there you have the root of the potential problem. When we, as business leaders come with set expectations of how things will run, how staff will behave, how client's needs will be met, our lives become about managing outcomes to meet those expectations.

I'm not suggesting that we don't have standards for the conduct of business. However, it's crucial that we acknowledge the culture of fear, greed and corruption that has informed and transformed what should be healthy expectancy into unhealthy and often unrealistic expectations.

We all carry measures of brokenness that subconsciously dictate what we expect of others. If we have been hurt or let down (and who hasn't?), our subconscious expectation may be that others will not do the right thing by us and our business. If we don't address our brokenness, we risk poisoning the well and reaping the very thing we want to avoid.

As I said in the introduction to this book, the prevailing business culture assumes the worst of people. People, instead of tasks, get managed and they 'do the right thing' out of fear of losing their job rather than because they're invested in the success of the company.

Fear-based leadership (if you can call it leadership) relies on a carrot and stick approach, bullying people and breeding uncertainty that is meant to keep people in line. The problem is that if you sow fear, you will reap fear, and when you assume the worst of people, you will probably get it.

LEADING OTHERS FOR SUCCESS

My definition of success these days is pretty much the opposite of when I started in business. Where once it was about accumulating possessions and proving myself, it's now about helping others achieve their God-given potential. I discovered the joy in championing the success of others and helping them soar. My mentality became – if I can do it for my employees, I have succeeded. Even more radically, it's about allowing others to stand on my shoulders and watching them fly higher than I ever could. What it came down to was that I had to lay down my agenda for God's plan.

Stop for a moment and let that sink in. How do you feel about providing a platform for others to soar higher than you? If you have a relationship with God, how do you feel about laying down your agenda for His? It's never a one-time deal. Being in a relationship with God means He gets to show me where I have deviated from His heart and when I'm not providing opportunities for others to soar. It's a humbling experience.

We must be deliberate in flipping the culture of greed, fear and corruption on its head by refusing to participate in it. That's the thing. It takes a conscious decision. We can't pretend that there is any other way that will lead to change. We have to refuse to feed the beast and then go another way. None of this was 'natural' to me. I had to learn how to lead with a sense of expectancy rather than the expectations that governed my business decisions for decades.

Let me reassure you. It's as hard as it sounds. Everything I knew was turned on its head. The only way I found that worked was to surrender to God and become a vessel that He could move in and through. It was a turning point for my entire life, not just the way I did business. It was hard, but let me assure you, it is worth it. It is completely worth it!

I believe there's a spiritual form of success that we don't talk about in business. It's the antithesis of fear, greed and corruption because life and generosity are its starting point. It only comes when we humble ourselves before God and submit to His plans and purposes rather than trying to get Him to approve of our brilliant ideas.

There is a precept about the fear of the Lord being the beginning of wisdom. It appears in Proverbs – also known as the Book of Wisdom – penned by King Solomon. I love the way that Brian Simmons puts it in The Passion Translation of Proverbs;

> The starting point for acquiring wisdom is to be consumed
> with awe as you worship Jehovah-God. To receive the
> revelation of the Holy One, you must come to the one
> who has living-understanding. Proverbs 9:10 The Passion
> Translation (TPT)

If we want to know the best way to go, we must come to the one who knows the best way – who has "living-understanding". My recipe for spiritual success is to humble myself before God to find out what He wants me to do and then do it.

It's what Jesus did.

> So Jesus said, "I speak to you timeless truth. The Son is
> not able to do anything from Himself or through my own

initiative. I only do the works that I see the Father doing, for the Son does the same works as his Father.

Because the Father loves his Son so much, he always reveals to me everything that he is about to do. And you will all be amazed when he shows me even greater works than what you've seen so far!"
John 5:19-20 The Passion Translation (TPT)

The good news is that God is eager to work with us!

"Call to Me and I will answer you, and I will tell you great and mighty things, which you do not know." Jeremiah 33:3 New American Standard Bible (NASB)

This is what it is to do business with God, and it's the best way I've found. As I've already shared, it's the only reason Network Neighborhood existed. When God starts something, He completes it, even when we make mistakes along the way. The prophet Micah summed it up;

He has told you, O man, what is good; And what does the Lord require of you but to do justice, to love kindness, and to walk humbly with your God? Micah 6:8 New American Standard Bible (NASB)

Trust me; there will be naysayers. There will always be those who don't believe that you've changed, who assume it's for show or a scam or that it's not possible to change the culture at a societal level.

We'll go into how to help your team success plans later in the chapter, but as the leader of my company, I had to implement fundamental changes that required me to model them before I could ask others to follow suit.

I gave certain people in the company permission to speak into my world whenever they felt the need. It wasn't fun, and it wasn't easy – for them or me. I had a reputation for tearing through people who weren't living up to my expectations or meeting what I considered to be reasonable demands. I had a lot to learn, and I did it in front of my team.

We live in a world of disruptive technologies; many of them are forces for good. I believe that one of the most significant disruptive innovations or 'technologies' we can engage in is unconditional love. Unconditional love that brings with it unconditional forgiveness and leads us to be dangerously transparent. If we give ourselves to this radical love, the world will change.

I've found that the only way to fully engage with this disruptive idea is to connect with the source of radical, unconditional love. Unless I receive, accept and absorb this love, my attempts to love others will be exhausting at best and unsustainable for any length of time. Unconditional love, forgiveness and dangerous transparency require vulnerability on my part. This love must first have its way in me. Unless I allow God, the source of infinite and unrelenting love, to love me – I don't know how I could ever be in a position to love others unconditionally.

Again, it's not about getting it right all the time; it's about being on the journey, staying humble, accountable and vulnerable to God and those He has brought alongside me to walk with me. As I do this, my definitions of failure and success come into line with His. As I find my success in being His child, His son that He delights in – I am free to help others discover their success in Him. As they soar, I soar and vice versa. It's about trading my perspective for God's perspective. It's about being seated with

Christ in heavenly places and doing business His way. Trust me; it's the only way to fly.

PERSPECTIVE

When I was a kid, there was a show on TV called Mr Squiggle. The star was a marionette called Mr Squiggle who lived on the moon and had a pencil for a nose. The highlight of the show was what Mr Squiggle did with his pencil nose. Children from around Australia would send in 'squiggles' for him to transform into pictures, which was the premise of the program. The premise was simple but profound and kept generations of kids spellbound. He always managed to turn the squiggles into a picture, but invariably the images were upside down or sideways. There was often more than one picture within the drawing and more than one way to view it. The final image revealed itself as Mr Squiggle's assistant turned the page the right way up.

I was thinking about Mr Squiggle the other day, and it struck me that it sums up the way I feel about how we teach business. Generations have been told that there is only one way to view and do business, even though the statistics show that the majority of companies fail in the first five to ten years.

Flipping the culture requires a fundamental shift of perspective. Businesses should be designed to be a blessing. Companies should add value by creating jobs, prospering individuals and families, enhancing the local community and benefiting society.

It's all about perspective. The culture of competing instead of completing skews perspectives towards winning and losing. Many people end up either as victims of a system or with an exaggerated sense of entitlement. You don't have to look hard to find examples of those who believe that they are winners and so should win – the entitlement mentality is often breathtaking in its boldness! By the same token, when people feel victimised, the outworking is just as damaging. Grumbling, gossip and division accompany both. They are the offspring of pride and all killers.

WORDS MATTER

Clear communication is vital in flipping the culture. Equally important are the words we choose to use in our contact with others. I have a massive problem with the adage, "Sticks and stones may break my bones, but words can never harm me." Quite frankly, that's a load of rubbish! I agree with the writer of Proverbs that life and death are found in the power of the tongue;

> Your words are so powerful that they will kill or give
> life, and the talkative person will reap the consequences.
> Proverbs 18:21 The Passion Translation (TPT)

Far from being benign, words matter. Our choice of words can open people up or shut them down. All of us have been affected by the words of others. It is part of the human condition. I read recently that for every negative comment, it takes five positive ones to erase the impact (Zenger and Folkman, 2015).

Humility opens the door for compassion to season our communication. There is a way to hold people to account that allows them dignity and provides a way to rectify the situation. So often the communication that occurs between bosses, managers and staff involves degrees of humiliation rather than humility.

I am guilty of the latter. I had to go on a journey around the way I communicate with others, particularly those in my employ. I had no problem holding people to account, but it would frequently end up with tears because I went about it all wrong.

My approach was, "You've had two weeks to get this finished; why isn't it done?" It's the perfect approach if you want to shut down healthy, respectful communication and ensure that the person on the receiving end is on the defensive!

Instead, I should have approached them with a genuine desire to understand what is happening that contributed to the situation. Something more like, "Hey, I see that this deadline has passed. What's going on in your world because this is unusual for you?"

The substantive difference between the two approaches is a relationship. The first approach requires no connection and is purely task-based. The preferred response to my employee involves a degree of relationship between us. It displays a level of understanding of their character, work ethic and life in general.

I had to learn, and believe me, it was as much an unlearning of old habits as it was learning new ways. I had to learn how to approach others with humility and gentleness while getting to the bottom of the issue. It took time, and as I've said, I had people around me who pointed out where I was messing up. No one is expecting us to be perfect, but we need to own when we aren't handling situations well and allow others to help us improve.

CREATING SUCCESS PLANS

Success plans were pivotal in transforming the culture of Network Neighborhood. In chapter five, we'll look at a few of the benefits that flowed from the introduction of company-wide planning. If you are prepared to be open, transparent and vulnerable with your team, bringing them on a journey, you have the potential to unite them in their passion for their work and unlock creativity in measures that will blow you away!

Success planning is for all levels of business; you, your company, staff and even your clients. It begins with you and your team coming together around the purpose, vision and mission of the business. It's about knowing and articulating your 'why', 'what', 'who' and 'how' and helping others to discover and articulate theirs. Remember, you are transforming an entire culture, so every level of the company will require attention.

Once you and your team have articulated the purpose, vision and mission of your business, it's time for the people. If you've been skimming over this section, I need you to stop now. I'm about to give you the critical component in the entire process. Creating success plans for people in your company will only work in the context of relationships. There must be a high degree of trust for your team to feel safe enough to participate freely in the process. That only comes through the deliberate development of relationships. So, if you don't want to get to know your staff, their hopes and dreams, their challenges and aspirations – maybe stop reading now.

Don't be surprised if people are initially sceptical. Given the toxic nature of many workplace cultures, people may be suspicious of bosses asking them to divulge their hopes, dreams and plans for the future. Be gentle with those who struggle to open up. They need to know that you aren't going to use the information gathered to manipulate or control. It sounds a bit melodramatic, but the fear is real! Your team need to feel your heart for them and experience your genuine desire to help them discover and live their own success. It's why you must go on the journey first and do so transparently. I keep harping on it because not doing it is the quickest way to derail the process for everybody else!

As I mentioned in chapter two, I decided to implement success plans for myself, my team and our clients after reading *The Big Five for Life*, by John Strelecky. I remember the day I announced we were going to embark on this journey. The staff looked at me like, "OK, here we go with another of Hugh's crazy ideas!" Then they found out I'd purchased five hundred copies of the book, realised I was serious, and to their credit went along for the ride!

Honestly, there were those who could not make the connection between creating success plans and the job they were employed to do. They were so accustomed to being a cog in the machine that they weren't able to take the leap. Then there were those who thought the whole thing was just plain weird! The latter, by and large, didn't stay or didn't make it past the initial job interview.

A wise person once said, "Never work on someone else's stuff more than they are prepared to work on it themselves." In the end, people are responsible for their choices and the degree to which they engage with both the process and the achievement of success.

WHAT WE DID!

The first step was to have everyone on the leadership team read *The Big Five for Life*. John Strelecky's book gave language to the journey I'd been on around my purpose in life, my vision, and mission. It's ultimately about discovering your 'why', 'what', 'who' and 'how'. We then started a conversation about our individual and corporate purposes. After articulating our purpose, we each developed a 'Big Five for Life' and settled on how we would measure success.

Here is what my success plan and 'Big Five for Life' looks like, as they appear on my email signature, business cards – pretty much any correspondence I send out!

Hugh Marquis

Marquis Developments

Purpose for Existence

To bring hope to the nations by helping people achieve their God-given potential

Big Five for Life

Leave the world a better place for me having been in it

Optimise creative opportunities

Visit every natural and man-made wonder of the world

Enhance lives through changing culture

Restore Kingdom principles to business

I know I need others to help me, so I added;

If you or anybody you know can help me achieve any of these, please contact me.

That sums me up, and I'm nothing if not forthright! I made no secret of my purpose or success plan because I knew I needed to be radically, some may say dangerously, transparent with my team if I expected them to open up and do the same.

It's no small thing to consider and articulate what success looks like for us. Some successes are based in our current stage of life, while others are for the much longer term. The process of getting to what was really, truly important to each was fascinating. When people finally presented their success plan, my first question was, "What would it mean if you weren't able to achieve this success?" If their response was, "Oh nothing much," which happened on more than one occasion, I sent them back to the drawing board. The lack of passion made it clear that they hadn't yet landed on what was driving or drawing them in life.

Stop for a moment. Can you identify what success looks like for you? Again, unless we are clear on our 'why' and 'what', it will be hard to put our finger on what success means to us, let alone 'how' we will get there and 'who' it will involve.

This next bit is significant. We honoured the time factor. You can't rush the process, no matter how much you may want to. It takes time and energy to formulate a success plan, share, refine and reshape where needed and finally settle on the finished document. As you can imagine, relationships deepened as people chose to be vulnerable and share their dreams.

What we did next was crucial. We set about crafting each person's working week to help them achieve their success. I'll talk more about that shortly. It's important to acknowledge that success plans are living documents with room to breathe and change over time. As people achieve one success, another will emerge. We discovered that people's idea of success evolved.

Once we worked through the process with leadership, we introduced the rest of our staff and all new employees to success planning.

HOW WE DID IT!

Let me walk you through the process for new employees. We would introduce the concept of success plans and 'The Big Five for Life' while discussing the ethos of NN during the interview.

As they came on board, the first week in the job included:

1. A meeting, outlining the starting salary and the six-monthly review based on their success plan rather than KPIs.

2. An overview of success plans and 'The Big Five for Life' before breaking it into two components so that they weren't overwhelmed.

   "We are going to have you look at and discover your purpose in life."

   "Once you know your purpose, what are the five things you need to do, be, and become for your purpose to be a reality?"

We helped them identify the big rocks needed to facilitate their 'why' and 'what'. We looked at the 'how' and the 'who' for each and created the pathway for achieving their 'Big Five'. It was a struggle for many to get their heads around a purpose and design for their lives that encompassed work, family, friends, recreation and rest. The most common question was, "What does this have to do with my job?"

This process usually took a couple of months, with regular meetings to help new team members discover, uncover or even rediscover their purpose in life. Some went along with the whole thing to tick boxes until they noticed that it worked! They found that success happens when you operate from your core values.

Alongside the one-on-one work, we ran team-wide training days to encourage staff in their journeys. That's one of the fun things about success plans – there is no one size fits all. My version of success works for me – but if everybody did things my way – it would have killed them! We are unique; wired for different types of success, with our personal path to walk. As a leader, I have the privilege of fostering unity while championing diversity.

Once trust was established, and team members accepted there was no hidden agenda behind success planning, it freed them to get serious about what it looked like for them. For some, success was about quality family time. A few staff members decided that success looked like three-day weekends. We talked. Why couldn't they do their work in four, ten-hour days? No reason? OK, so do that then! It was about creative solutions that worked for both staff and the company.

Every six months, the entire team would get together to review their success plans and discuss how their 'Big Five' were progressing. These times kicked vulnerability, transparency and accountability into high gear. You need a great deal of trust in the room for people to open up about where they're at in pursuing their purpose and creating successful lives.

There is no room for shame or guilt, only accountability as staff asked the questions of one another, "So what are you doing about your 'Big Five'?" If the response was, "Well nothing really", the push back was "Why not?". Again, it wasn't about shaming – but about championing each other's success.

One of our senior team was an avid golfer. His 'Big Five' included playing on every Masters golf course in the world. I asked him what it would take for this to become a reality, and it turned out that he needed to get his handicap down. How was he going to achieve it? As a group, we suggested that he play golf once a week.

I discovered that it's one thing for people to agree to and develop a success plan, but changing a culture is another thing altogether. It requires patience and perseverance. At his six-month review, he revealed that he wasn't playing golf anymore. "What happened?" I asked, to which he replied, "I've got too much work to do." The way he saw it, taking time out of his week to play golf was impeding his productivity. The way I saw it, he was allowing the busyness of work to rob him of his success. Productivity and busyness are not necessarily synonymous, so I challenged him on his thinking.

"I think that you're stealing from the company by not following through with your success plan," I countered.

"What?" he was incredulous, and I could see he was trying not to take offence. What I wanted him to understand was that his busyness did not equate to productivity and that our success as a company depended on all of us working towards our own goals.

After he thought about it, he said, "I don't get the fact that you want me to take time off for my success."

"I'm not actually saying that," I replied. "Why don't you take groups of staff out on golf mornings to build relationships? Or you could do the same for our clients." He could use his success plan to help transform the company culture and value our clients. That way, he was serving both his success and that of the company. All he needed was a change of perspective.

As I said earlier, success plans need to evolve with the changing life circumstances of people. One of our employees wanted to get married and have a family and made this one of his 'Big Five'. Happily, he achieved this while employed at Network Neighborhood. At one of our meetings, I challenged him. "OK, so you're now a husband and father. What does your success plan look like going forward? Is it about being the best husband and father you can and defining what that looks like for you?" Achieving one measure of success makes room for new and exciting adventures!

SUCCESS PLANS FOR CLIENTS AND SUPPLIERS

We were so pleased with the success plans we created both for the company and staff, that we began to brainstorm about how we could do the same for our clients. How could we serve them to the best of our ability according to their definition of success? Why would we do that? Because we wanted them to be successful. Their success was our success.

The first thing we did was engage in conversation with the school principals. We asked, "What does success look like for you in the way we serve you as our client?" Or, "What did you envisage when we installed the technology and set up the network?"

We tried not to make assumptions but to get them to tell us what success looked like for them in their school. We came with thoughts to contribute, but again, in the form of questions. Was it that every child had access to a device, be it a laptop or iPad from grade three upward? Was it that the school roll could be marked off on the network daily? Was it that they wanted to create a learning environment that set the primary school students up for success in secondary school?

Discussions started with principals and often widened to include leadership teams. The technology revolution was upon these school communities, and it was a privilege to serve them as they embraced it and made it work for their school communities. Once the vision for the school was defined, and we agreed on the measures of success, we worked closely together to see it through. Regular reviews were set up to assess whether we were achieving the success plan and to make any adjustments needed to stay on track.

Some of the schools welcomed the process, and we were able to help them take full advantage of the available technological advances. Others were overwhelmed with the enormity of the shift and struggled to cast a vision for their school community.

We were on a bit of a roll, so we started thinking about our suppliers. Granted, this was a bit trickier. How do you create success for your suppliers, given that you are the client? It's a great exercise to put yourself in the shoes of those with whom you do business and look at how you can model caring, sharing and prosperity for all. We considered what a successful relationship with our company would look like for them. What did us paying our bills on time look like for them? What did lines of credit, or moving stock look like for them?

As we implemented success plans for our suppliers, it cemented the relationships and unbeknownst to us, paved the way for them to come to our aid in our hour of need. More about that later!

THE BOTTOM LINE

The bottom line is that if we don't define what success and failure look like for us and our businesses, somebody else will. We need to be clear on our 'why', 'what', 'who' and 'how' if we are to avoid being defined by the expectations of a world steeped in pride.

When we choose to lead our teams with vulnerability and transparency, we are well on our way to creating a generous and righteous culture. It requires determination, persistence and patience with others as they get used to functioning in an environment that expects them to succeed but allows them to determine their success!

Remember, clear and consistent communication is vital when leading others for success; in word and deed. Your team need assurance that this isn't the latest management technique in a long line of purely profit-driven initiatives. Giving staff a voice and coming to the process with an expectancy that they will contribute in significant ways frees people and is a risk worth taking.

You be you and let your people be their unique selves. Take a stand against the fear of losing control that has ruled business culture for so long. Choose generosity and kindness consistently and watch what happens!

ACTION STEPS

It's time to think about where you are at right now. I've included some questions to help you process your thoughts. Can I encourage you to take some time to consider and record your answers?

1. Are you leading your staff and empowering them, or are you managing tasks and people?

2. What assumptions have you made about your staff, both positive and negative?

3. Are you projecting your insecurities onto others and making unreasonable demands?

4. Do you live with expectancy or do you have expectations of others that they must meet to gain your approval?

Open up a conversation with your staff and find out how they define 'failure' and 'success' in life and the business.

Talk openly together about what it looks like to daily embrace the core values of people above profits and completing rather than competing.

How can you introduce the concept of success plans for your staff? I strongly recommend you start by getting hold of John Strelecky's book *Big Five for Life*. (In case you are wondering, I don't gain financially from you buying John's book, I just think it's excellent!)

Find out more at https://www.johnstrelecky.com

In chapter five, we are going to talk about how to unlock and unleash the potential that lies within the people around you. It's one of my favourite things to do, so let's get to it!

CHAPTER FIVE

Unlocking and unleashing untapped resources

THE COST OF DOING BUSINESS

Think about where your business is at right now. What challenges are you facing? What opportunities are you considering? Have you been thinking about bringing in the 'right' people to help you overcome obstacles, grapple with problems and find solutions? Has your mind gone to the type of person you 'need' to take full advantage of the opportunities before you? Are you looking around at your current team and struggling to see how they can meet the demands of your business?

According to the Business Insider (Australia), "It has been estimated the real cost of recruitment in Australia can be upwards of 50 per cent of a person's salary." Furthermore, "the time it takes to hire more than doubled from 2010 to 2015, resulting in average productivity losses and recruitment costs of over $34,000. The fact is, retention pays. With younger generations far more likely to job-hop than older workers, retention is only getting harder. What makes a difference is training and reskilling" (Cairnes, 2018).

While I broadly agree, I would say that it's about more than providing existing employees with training and re-skilling opportunities. It's about discovering, unlocking and unleashing the creative potential that currently exists within your staff. It's about creating job descriptions that set people free rather than boxing them in, and it's about valuing people above profit. When we call out the gold in people and give them opportunities to bring solutions, to innovate and to create, on the whole, that's what they will do!

I keep talking about flipping the culture, and it's no exaggeration. Economics is, by definition, the study of the allocation of scarce resources. We are trying to run companies in a culture with a core belief of lack, of a limited pie. It doesn't take much imagination to see how greed, fear and corruption take root and flourish in this fertile ground!

The fear of lack, a poverty mindset, and the culture of winning at all costs infiltrate every aspect of businesses. People feel like cogs in a soulless machine and act accordingly; creativity and productivity drop, and loyalty goes out the window. And rightly so. People are not going to invest themselves in a company that considers them as replaceable (and reminds them of it!)

As I said at the beginning of this book, we have come to assume the worst of others. We expect to be taken advantage of, so we make sure we get in first. To instigate a change to a culture of generosity, we must acknowledge that this is the current state of affairs for much of the world. Then we need to recognise it in our businesses. It's not about judgment or shame; it's about a better way to live and do business.

This is where the rubber hits the road, and the real work of valuing people begins. If we dare to take our businesses from fear to outrageous favour, it has to start with us as leaders. We must pioneer a new way of being and doing. Each one of us has to live and walk the journey we are asking others to take.

It's not going to happen overnight, and not everyone is going to jump on board straight away. Some may never see or accept the benefits. It's incredibly tempting to believe that there is the 'perfect' employee out there just waiting to slot seamlessly into our businesses and give us the edge we've been missing.

I'm not suggesting that people never leave and I'm not talking about necessary changes where there is an obvious mismatch between employee and company. There must be provisions for releasing people – under the right circumstances and in the best possible way. It's not always achievable – but that's no reason not to set the bar high.

Why do we go for the quick fix? Why do so many choose to parachute people into positions believing they will be the answer to their prayers? What I've experienced in my business and witnessed in other organisations is that the pervading culture drives us to find the 'competitive edge' and dictates the hiring and firing of staff. I also know that while it may be easy to diagnose, it's hard to avoid. I know because I fell back into the status quo while leading Network Neighborhood – where we had already flipped the culture and were reaping the harvest!

Ultimately, I believe business is about prospering and providing for the welfare of the whole of society. So what does that look like when it comes to making the most of the human, social and financial capital residing in your business?

One of the things I love about Jesus is the way he believes in people. He hung around with a pretty motley crew, who let Him down with almost monotonous regularity. And He refused to give up on them. Take Peter, for example. He declares that Jesus is the Son of God, making grandiose statements about his loyalty – even to death – and then deserts Jesus in His time of greatest need.

What does Jesus do? He continues to call the gold out in Peter, allowing him to step into his destiny. He restored His relationship with Peter on the shores of the very lake where their friendship began and commissioned him to lead the church!

> After they had breakfast, Jesus said to Peter, "Simon, son of John, do you burn with love for me more than these?"
>
> Peter answered, "Yes, Lord! You know that I have great affection for you!"
>
> "Then take care of my lambs," Jesus said.
>
> Jesus repeated his question the second time, "Simon, son of John, do you burn with love for me?"
>
> Peter answered, "Yes, my Lord! You know that I have great affection for you!"
>
> "Then take care of my sheep," Jesus said.
>
> Then Jesus asked him again, "Peter, son of John, do you have great affection for me?"
>
> Peter was saddened by being asked the third time and said, "My Lord, you know everything. You know that I burn with love for you!"
>
> Jesus replied, "Then feed my lambs! Peter, listen, when you were younger you made your own choices and you went where you pleased. But one day when you are old, others wil tie you up and escort you where you would not choose to go – and you will spread out your arms." (Jesus said this to Peter as a prophecy of what kind of death he would die, for the glory of God.) And then he said, "Peter, follow me!"
> John 21:15-19 The Passion Translation (TPT)

Jesus has done the same for me. He believes in me and has given me opportunities to step up – even though I have stuffed up time and again. He knows that He has my "Yes" and has never given up on me. As a result, I have been unleashed creatively in ways I could never have dreamed or imagined!

What would it look like for you to unleash the human, social and financial capital that's already in your business? Our human condition lends itself to believing that if we just had access to that financial capital, those particular people, or that specific process – everything would change in our favour.

My question is, what if everything we need is already at our fingertips, and all we require are the tools to unlock the creative potential that resides in our business? Which leads to further questions. What if we choose to see our company, our staff, every aspect of our business through the eyes of God? What if we allow the Holy Spirit to shift our perspective on the state of our organisations? What does God have to say about the human, social and financial capital that exists right now in your business?

In a culture focussed on economic resources and capital, we have the opportunity to focus on people. We can align ourselves with the things that are important to God, knowing that He is faithful to supply all our needs according to His riches in glory (Philippians 4:19). Alternatively, we can align ourselves with a culture of lack, of winners and losers, of competition. Trust me; there will never be enough of what we seek to satisfy our need.

I believe there is more than enough money in the world. When we make financial acquisition our primary focus, it will always be a story of diminishing returns. Why? Because we fail to recognise our most valuable capital; human and social. If you unlock and unleash people, I know you will be shocked at how the financial capital will flow. As an aside, have you noticed that when people continuously focus on money and cash flow in their business – it's rarely positive? It's more often about lack than the blessings encountered.

Money is a tool. It should be there to facilitate and fund – not as an end in itself or a way to gain power over others. Jesus warned us of the consequences of buying into the culture of pride.

> "How could you worship two gods at the same time? You will have to hate one and love the other, or be devoted to one and despise the other. You can't worship the true God while enslaved to the god of money!" Matthew 6:24 The Passion Translation (TPT)

So how do you discover, unlock and unleash the potential of your employees? It sounds like the right thing to do, but what does it look like practically and how does it work in the day-to-day running of your business?

In this chapter, we are going to walk through how to unleash the potential that is already in your team. I'm going to give you practical steps to help you build creative environments that are solution focussed.

HUMAN, SOCIAL AND FINANCIAL CAPITAL

How do you tap into the existing creativity of your people and train, equip, empower and release them to soar?

It starts with your company's 'Why', 'What', 'Who' and 'How'. They must be front and centre and revisited regularly by the whole team. The question to ask initially is, "Have we stayed true to the vision and mission or have we been diverted into areas that are competing with our 'Why' and 'What'?"

It requires vulnerability, transparency and accountability from everybody. It's not about assigning blame to individuals. It's about resetting where needed so that the main thing stays the main thing. When people are not put on the defensive by leadership, you will be surprised at how willing they are to own their mistakes or admit to where they have gone a little off track. It becomes about helping each other make necessary tweaks and allows the creativity of the team to come to the fore with solutions.

For far too long, we have allowed financial capital to be the marker of success for business. It's time to value the human and social capital that creates wealth in the first place.

HUMAN CAPITAL

People are your most valuable resource. More than that, they are precious individuals created in the image of God with a purpose that only they can fulfil. As leaders in business, we need to value people over profit. Without people – there is no profit – so why on earth would we prize the inanimate over the welfare of those whose creativity is the spark of the divine.

In the end, words are cheap and meaningless if they aren't followed up with action. At Network Neighborhood, we valued our team, and put our money where our mouth was. Success plans were both tangible and practical ways of acknowledging the uniqueness of our team members and supporting their dreams. We also had an expectancy of the valuable contribution they would make across the company and our job descriptions that were a testament to that ethos.

Again, my role as an employer is to look after the welfare and wellbeing of my staff. If I help meet their needs and foster their development, it frees people to bring their best to work, every day. It's more than checking in on how they are doing and monitoring everybody's stress levels. It's about working together to achieve a vision. It's about giving them a voice in how we go about it and an opportunity to contribute in significant ways to realising the mission and vision. It's about setting yourself, your employees and your business up for success.

SOCIAL CAPITAL

When I talk about 'social capital' I'm referring to a couple of different things. For me, it's firstly about recognising, harnessing and releasing the social capital that exists within my business. If I choose to value the human capital and focus on completing instead of competing, I set my team up for super-charged collaboration. 'Make Me Better' sessions were designed to foster the social capital in the company, and they worked a treat!

Secondly, 'social capital' for Network Neighborhood included our clients; the school network and more broadly, the education system in Australia. From the outset, our vision was to have every student with a computing device that connected to a school network, regardless of their financial capacity. Our vision and mission were, therefore, more about serving the school community and developing systems to implement strategies than about selling goods and services. Our vision complemented and supported the vision of the school communities we served, and we operated in a solution-based market place.

Honestly, I think we innately operated with social capital in mind but didn't necessarily articulate it. I'd not seen an example of the solution-based market place before. I was used to a competitive market place, with winners and losers, but providing solutions felt right. From the outset, we were about transforming society through the education of children. As we fumbled and stumbled our way through, the acknowledgement and development of social capital became part of our core ethos.

FINANCIAL CAPITAL

I like to think of financial capital as 'putting your money where your mouth is'. The bottom line is that you need to invest financially in your people.

I was attending the conference of a plumbing and electrical franchise in my hometown of Melbourne a few years back. My friend Steve was presenting on investing in training and development for staff and was asked this question by one of the franchise owners.

"But what if I spend money and time training my people and they leave?"

Steve's response was perfect, "What if you don't, and they stay?"

It's a valid question and one that many business owners ask. We all want a return on our investment, and any time we invest in others, we are vulnerable. Vulnerability has become a dirty word in business. Being vulnerable is almost always viewed in the negative. How often do we hear that a company has made itself vulnerable to this or that terrible fate? The truth is that vulnerability is how we build genuine relationships. We can't truly invest in others without taking a risk.

What's the alternative? If we don't invest in people, we perpetuate a toxic culture. We let fear win. We risk shutting down the very people we rely on to invest in our companies day in and day out. I believe it's a false economy. We save a few dollars and deprive ourselves of loyal staff whose creativity is the key to developing our financial bottom line.

JOB DESCRIPTIONS THAT SET PEOPLE FREE

In a traditional business model, job descriptions segment and silo. They carve companies up into discrete parts and divide tasks amongst staff. Managers are appointed to manage the people doing the tasks so that the business succeeds. People receive enough information to do their work (hopefully), but not enough to contribute meaningfully beyond that. They get a tiny piece of the pie, and their job becomes as much about protecting their morsel as it is about working for the good of the company.

At Network Neighborhood, we wanted everyone working for the good of the company and able to contribute as broadly as possible. Our job descriptions were, therefore, light in detail. The most important criterium was the one that's at the bottom of most job descriptions:

Any other duty you need to perform to make the job work.

Of course, there were individual roles with tasks assigned; otherwise, anarchy would ensue! The difference was that our staff had their eye on the big picture and were willing to work collaboratively across the company to accomplish our vision. In my opinion, restricting people to one area is cutting off your nose to spite your face!

It flew in the face of a culture that manages people instead of tasks. As I shared in chapter two, we copped criticism from those who ascribed to the status quo and individual KPIs. All I can tell you is that it worked. We built trust and an atmosphere of safety that freed the team to find solutions for our clients.

JOB DESCRIPTIONS AND SUCCESS PLANS: DO THEY WORK TOGETHER?

Do job descriptions and success plans complement each other? Are they ever at odds? The short answer is, it depends. It depends on how you've structured your company and the underlying ethos. You can't just create success plans for your staff and expect them to work if you haven't addressed the culture. You can't expect a culture that fosters fear and competition to support an initiative based on caring, sharing and prosperity for all.

Let me explain what happened at Network Neighborhood.

When we started the company, our job descriptions were loose, as were our success plans. That's because we were about doing things as a family. We worked together and looked out for one another. Job descriptions and success plans worked hand in hand.

Things changed drastically when we went through our 'dark night of the soul'. This was when we employed managers who instituted individualised job descriptions and KPI. The whole idea of success plans hinges on a culture of generosity. The culture we introduced created individualism and siloed the staff. Job descriptions became about the task instead of the bigger picture. We didn't scrap success plans; they just faded into the background and became irrelevant in the new reality.

I've been asked on many occasions what alerted me to the negative impact of our cultural changes. That's easy. People started leaving. Staff turnover at NN was almost non-existent before we made the changes and 'suddenly' a few months after the shift of culture people felt the need to move on.

When I came to my senses and tried to recover our culture, I sought to reinstate success plans. It was hard. The comment

I heard most was, "Why should I trust the leadership?" We lost the trust of the team, and once you've lost that element, it's a long, steep road back.

The first thing I did was apologise to the staff. I had to take ownership of a lousy decision. All I could do was be upfront and admit that I got it wrong. Never fun; but necessary if we were ever going to move forward. Next, I had to reframe the culture, to remind us of what we had before and commit to finding a way back to the culture of completing, generosity and prosperity for all.

The consequence of our misstep was that some of the staff didn't want to come on the journey with us. They felt betrayed and needed to move on.

The bottom line is that job descriptions and success plans should complement one another. That is only possible in a culture that values people over profit and believes that the welfare of staff is central to the success of the business.

UNLOCKING RESOURCES AND UNLEASHING CREATIVITY

How well do you know the people who work in your company? The beauty of creating success plans for staff is that you get to know their core values, what drives them and what their aspirations are for the future. Along the way, you also get to uncover hidden talents and passions. I know I sound like a stuck record – but it's all about relationships!

Until we invest time and energy into our teams, we won't know what gems are hiding in plain sight. You may well discover that success for your staff includes taking your business to heights that you never imagined.

Creativity is in our DNA. It's an essential part of being human because we're created in the image of the Creator.

Let's take a look at Genesis and the creation story.

THE CREATION

In the beginning God created the heavens and the earth.
The earth was formless and void, and darkness was over the
surface of the deep, and the Spirit of God was moving over
the surface of the waters. Then God said, "Let there be light";
and there was light. God saw that the light was good; and God
separated the light from the darkness. God called the light day,
and the darkness He called night. And there was evening and
there was morning, one day.

Then God said, "Let there be an expanse in the midst of the
waters, and let it separate the waters from the waters." God
made the expanse, and separated the waters which were below
the expanse from the waters which were above the expanse; it
was so. God called the expanse heaven. And there was evening
and there was morning, a second day.

Then God said, "Let the waters below the heavens be gathered
into one place, and let the dry land appear"; and it was so.
God called the dry land earth, and the gathering of the waters
He called seas; and God saw that it was good. Then God said,
"Let the earth sprout vegetation, plants yielding seed, and
fruit trees on the earth bearing fruit after their kind with seed
in them"; and it was so. The earth brought forth vegetation,
plants yielding seed after their kind, and trees bearing fruit
with seed in them, after their kind; and God saw that it was
good. There was evening and there was morning, a third day.

Then God said, "Let there be lights in the expanse of the
heavens to separate the day from the night, and let them

be for signs and for seasons and for days and years; and let them be for lights in the expanse of the heavens to give light on the earth"; and it was so. God made the two great lights, the greater light to govern the day, and the lesser light to govern the night; He made the stars also. God placed them in the expanse of the heavens to give light on the earth, and to govern the day and the night, and to separate the light from the darkness; and God saw that it was good. There was evening and there was morning, a fourth day.

Then God said, "Let the waters teem with swarms of living creatures, and let birds fly above the earth in the open expanse of the heavens." God created the great sea monsters and every living creature that moves, with which the waters swarmed after their kind, and every winged bird after its kind; and God saw that it was good. God blessed them, saying, "Be fruitful and multiply, and fill the waters in the seas, and let birds multiply on the earth." There was evening and there was morning, a fifth day.

Then God said, "Let the earth bring forth living creatures after their kind: cattle and creeping things and beasts of the earth after their kind"; and it was so. God made the beasts of the earth after their kind, and the cattle after their kind, and everything that creeps on the ground after its kind; and God saw that it was good.

Then God said, "Let Us make man in Our image, according to Our likeness; and let them rule over the fish of the sea and over the birds of the sky and over the cattle and over all the earth, and over every creeping thing that creeps on the earth." God created man in His own image, in the image of God He created him; male and female He created them. God blessed them; and God said to them, "Be fruitful and multiply, and

fill the earth, and subdue it; and rule over the fish of the sea and over the birds of the sky and over every living thing that moves on the earth." Then God said, "Behold, I have given you every plant yielding seed that is on the surface of all the earth, and every tree which has fruit yielding seed; it shall be food for you; and to every beast of the earth and to every bird of the sky and to everything that moves on the earth which has life, I have given every green plant for food"; and it was so. God saw all that He had made, and behold, it was very good. And there was evening and there was morning, the sixth day.
Genesis 1 (NASB)

I love this story of the ongoing expression of God's creativity. The creativity that set the cosmos in motion cannot be contained. Everything about God is creative. The essence of life is creativity and life itself is the evidence of creativity. We are created in the image of the One who is creativity and whose creativity has no limits. As image bearers of this Creator – why do we limit our ability to be creative? How can we possibly define what is and what is not possible when we look at the infinite creativity of God?

As I read the narrative, something else I notice is the distinct lack of stress involved the act of creation. The universe was born out of the breath and the word of God. It was born in and from joy and peace and power. I love to imagine the conversations between Father God, Jesus and the Holy Spirit at the end of each 'day'. I love that they stopped (being outside time notwithstanding!) and took 'time' to reflect on their handiwork, enjoying all that they had accomplished.

I'm convinced that we place false limits on our creativity, allowing pressures of our own making to stifle and squash creativity.

TO EVERYTHING THERE IS A SEASON

No one can sustain creativity in a space permeated by greed, fear and corruption; they are the very antithesis of creativity.

I believe that there is a time for ideas to come forth in the world. Stop for a moment and consider the crazy concept of flight. What I find fascinating is that while the notion of people flying had been in our consciousness for hundreds, if not thousands, of years; there were fifty years during which people from all around the world began to develop and test technology to enable mankind to achieve heavier-than-air, powered, and controlled flight. From New Zealand to France, Germany to America, the race was on to see who could pull it off. Why? Because it was an idea whose time had come.

I am convinced that we have access to heavenly storehouses containing blueprints and solutions for every challenge, every obstacle, to cure every disease. We have access to a largely untapped resource – the wisdom of Heaven – but I don't think that many of us really believe it. My personal experience and those of many others I come into contact with attest to God's desire to share ideas and knowledge with those whose ear is inclined and heart yielded. Again, the culture of pride thrives on the concept of finite resources with everyone scrambling to secure their scrap. Why do we buy into it when the evidence of our limitless God surrounds us?

The storehouse of ideas is not just about resources; it's also about people and relationships. Sometimes we'll encounter situations that we don't know how to address. There are challenges that we have not faced before, situations we have never seen. We can ASK! We can say to the Lord, "Is there wisdom that you have for me, a strategy that can apply in people's lives?" Some call it prophetic. Some call it discernment, others call it words of knowledge.

It reminds me of King Solomon's encounter with God,

In Gibeon the Lord appeared to Solomon in a dream at night; and God said, "Ask what you wish Me to give you."

SOLOMON'S PRAYER

Then Solomon said, "You have shown great lovingkindness to Your servant David my father, according as he walked before You in truth and righteousness and uprightness of heart toward You; and You have reserved for him this great lovingkindness, that You have given him a son to sit on his throne, as it is this day. Now, O Lord my God, You have made Your servant king in place of my father David, yet I am but a little child; I do not know how to go out or come in. Your servant is in the midst of Your people which You have chosen, a great people who are too many to be numbered or counted. So give Your servant an understanding heart to judge Your people to discern between good and evil. For who is able to judge this great people of Yours?"

GOD'S ANSWER

It was pleasing in the sight of the Lord that Solomon had asked this thing. God said to him, "Because you have asked this thing and have not asked for yourself long life, nor have asked riches for yourself, nor have you asked for the life of your enemies, but have asked for yourself discernment to understand justice, behold, I have done according to your words. Behold, I have given you a wise and discerning heart, so that there has been no one like you before you, nor shall one like you arise after you. 1 Kings 3:5-12 (NASB)

God knows how to call the gold up in people. We need to tap into that. We need the wisdom that comes from Him if we are to add value and call out the gold in the lives of people around us.

THE MONTARA CIRCLE

When we understand that we have access to solutions from Heaven to address the human, social and financial aspects of any problem, we are well on the way to creating a legacy far more significant than we can imagine.

In 2011, David Batstone from the Not for Sale Campaign came across a problem in need of a solution. He called together fifty thought and business leaders from around the world to what became known as the Montara Circle. We all arrived in Montara, Southern California, and Dave presented the problem.

He asked us to come up with a solution to a serious problem facing one community in Peru. In his capacity as co-founder and president of the global anti-slavery organisation, Dave visited a small, impoverished community nestled on the banks of the Amazon River. This tiny settlement was located six hours down-river from the nearest town with sufficient infrastructure to provide education for the children of the village. The children would travel the six hours up-river at the start of each week and return the following weekend. The big problem was that when the kids landed in town, there was no one to stay with, no protection for them, leaving them vulnerable to exploitation and trafficking.

The only agenda for the meeting was to come up with an innovative solution that addressed the human, social and financial needs of the community in a sustainable and financially viable way. Over two days, we formed working groups, collaborated on each other's ideas and eventually voted on a solution. What we came up with was an idea called Smart Tea using produce from the local area and supplied by local people. Smart Tea later morphed into a company called REBBL, which stands for Roots, Extracts, Berry, Bark and Leaves. It's an entirely commercial business with a $20 million turnover producing a drink awarded BevNET's Best New Product of 2016 and Best Functional Beverage of 2015 (REBBL, 2019). The village now has schools, healthcare centres, accommodation and more. The community also own boats able to transport people safely to the larger towns, significantly reducing the risk of trafficking and exploitation.

All of this came out of one man's determination to seek a better way for one community. It's what is possible when we tap into the heart of God and let Him set the agenda. Imagine what He can do through you, your family, your staff, and your business to change the lives of others!

WHEN PEOPLE LEAVE

And so, we come to the pointy end of the stick. All of this unlocking, unleashing and releasing the creativity of our employees is fine and dandy until they get a better offer and leave!

If we want, we can live believing that we have control over people. We can try to exert that control by refusing to invest in them and by managing them through KPIs that silo and discourage creative solutions. My question is, what kind of workplace do we create in the process? I know I've said it over and over, but in the end, life is about relationships. The genuine ones always involve an element of risk.

Social researcher, Brené Brown, Ph.D., LMSW has a lot to say about vulnerability and is convinced it's an essential trait for those who want to lead well.

> *"The courage to be vulnerable is not about winning or losing, it's about the courage to show up when you can't predict or control the outcome."* (Brown, 2018)

When we operate within the culture and under the influence of pride, it's all about managing resources and tasks rather than developing relationships and finding and releasing the gold in others. It's about us, the bottom line of finances and getting what we consider to be a significant return.

Hear me on this. Greed, fear and corruption are in direct opposition to unlocking, unleashing and potentially releasing employees out of your workplace. If you want to embrace a generous culture of caring, sharing and prosperity for all – you must be willing to release people and bless them on their way out.

Let's take the bull by the horns and go to the 'worst case' scenario. One of your most valuable employees, a person you have poured your life into and who has been unlocked and unleashed creatively, now has the opportunity to step into a higher position at a new company.

You both know that it's because of the investment in them that they are ready to take on a more demanding role. Or perhaps they are stepping out to pursue their own vision and mission. When you raise people up, help them cast a vision for their lives, and set them up for success – some will leave. It's a natural outworking of prosperity for all.

On the whole, we had very few people leave Network Neighborhood. However, there were times when fantastic people moved on. I recall the conversation when Ray, a valued member of staff, came to me.

"Hugh, I've been offered this COO role. I love working here, but I get the chance to create this culture in that workplace."

I mean, what can you say to that? I was sad to see Ray leave and would love for him to have stayed at NN, but I wanted to know how we could help him go in the best way possible. More than that, I wanted to ensure there was an open door for people like Ray to return should the opportunity arise down the track.

I think that leaders often make one big mistake when good people tell them they are going to move on. They offer them more money to stay. My question is – why isn't the company already paying them at that level if they're worth it? It's a fear-based response that attempts to exert power through the control of finances. It's this toxic culture that only values great people when there is the prospect of losing the advantage that they bring.

I want to be known as an employer who champions people, period! I'd rather raise people up, and 'risk' releasing those who have caught the caring, sharing, prosperity for all culture of generosity. The alternative is to preside over a company of people who feel unappreciated, used and unable to contribute to the best of their ability.

THE BOTTOM LINE

If there is one thing I want you to get from this book, it's that there is more to your business than the business you do. Your business is about so much more than providing a product or service to a client. It's about more than providing for your family or creating a lifestyle of ease. It's even about more than the fulfilment of your dreams and passions. You have the opportunity and privilege to positively impact the lives of your team, their families and beyond. There is a world out there that you can help change for the better.

Our job is to unlock and unleash the creativity around us so that everyone benefits. The more we practice this within our businesses, the more opportunities we'll encounter beyond our companies to bring solutions that aren't just out of the box, they leave the box behind! And you know what, it's fun! Investing in people is one of the most fun things I've ever done! Not that it's easy, but the joy of helping to lift communities out of poverty, of protecting children from being trafficked and of doing it with others in and through our businesses is worth every ounce of effort.

I want you and your business to experience outrageous favour. What I've discovered is that being favoured has a lot to do with the extent to which we extend favour. We reap what we sow. As much as I have championed others, I have received more than I could ever have asked or imagined. For those questioning the merit and wisdom of it, favour is not about allowing yourself to be taken advantage of, and it's not about blindly promoting people. Showing favour is about calling the gold out in others and allowing them to rise and shine. There is accountability because it takes place in the context of relationship. For me, extending favour is as much about my relationship with God as it is with others. When the Holy Spirit prompts me to show favour to another person, who am I to say "No"?

If you will take the time to invest in your team, call the gold out and unleash them within your business – you will see a return on your investment in multiple ways. I'm excited for you and your business as you uncover the hidden gems that lie just beneath the surface.

ACTION STEPS

Below are a bunch of questions to help you identify and begin to release the gold;

1. Can you identify the untapped human, social and financial capital that currently exists in your business and networks?

2. What skills and talents are lying dormant in your team that, with some investment from you, could enhance your business and bring the best out in them?

3. Why not have a round-table discussion with your staff about the skills and talents they want to unleash within the business?

4. If you have a relationship with God, take some time to pray and ask Him to give you insight into the gold that currently resides in the people in your business.

5. If you don't have a relationship with God, I'd love to invite you to connect with the source of creativity. What have you got to lose? Jesus said that all we have to do is ask, and we will receive. I promise you, connecting with Him is easily the best decision you will ever make in your life.

JOB DESCRIPTIONS

It's time to challenge the status quo. Take some time over the coming week to review the roles within your company. Below are some questions and activities to get the ball rolling.

1. How do you view job descriptions?

2. Has your perspective on the role of job descriptions changed?

3. Have a look at the job descriptions in your company. Do they silo people, separating them from others, or do they set them free to contribute in a way that lifts the entire business?

4. Have you ever asked your employees what they think of their job descriptions? It's a great place to start if you want to unlock and unleash untapped creativity in your staff.

5. This week why not start the ball rolling with your team. Give your team some time to think about what they would change and then follow up with a round-table discussion in the following week.

6. Ask your team to evaluate their current job descriptions.

7. If you want to take it to the next level, ask them what they would add to their job descriptions to help them contribute more broadly to the success of the company.

In chapter six, we are going to talk about some of the pitfalls of success and how to ride the wave of favour. We'll also look at what to do when everything hits the fan, and how to refire and restart if things fall apart.

CHAPTER SIX

Survivor's guide to riding the wave

How are you doing? Are you feeling excited? Scared? Sceptical? All of the above? In this chapter, we'll talk about how to lead while riding the wave of transition. How to survive the highs, the lows, and launch out the other side not only surviving but thriving. Let's not beat about the bush. Change can be hard. Organisational change is hard. Cultural change is seriously hard work. While it may be tempting to skip some of the steps and overlay the old framework with a new one – unless we deal with the fundamentals – old habits will die hard and any changes made will likely fall at the first hurdle.

The vast majority of us have lived and worked in toxic cultures, where we were treated as tasks to be managed, rather than people to be creatively unlocked and unleashed. Too many of us have had that squirming feeling when a co-worker is humiliated in front of the team. We may even have been on the receiving end of bullying tactics used by managers who don't know any other way to get the job done. Like it or not, we are dealing with generations of damaged people who expect to be shafted by management, blamed and shamed for their mistakes, and not given credit for their achievements.

Changing a toxic culture – even in one company – is kind of like trying to turn an aircraft carrier around when it's going at full speed! That particular feat takes an average radius of five nautical miles to achieve with up to seventy people involved in the process! Even if you've gathered your team and worked on your purpose, vision and mission, it's going to take time, grace, patience, kindness, vulnerability, transparency and accountability to help people make the transition.

There's also the reality that if we aren't careful, we can be taken out by our success! We are going to look at the red flags, red herrings and pitfalls that can lead to either success or failure and why it's crucial that we are clear on what success looks like for us.

Perspective is everything. When we view our businesses through the lens of a higher vision with a mission that supports it, success and failure take on very different meanings. In particular, it changes our mindset around failure. When we understand our 'why', 'what', 'who' and 'how' – the business becomes a vehicle through which we accomplish the vision but not the end in itself.

REVISITING FAILURE AND SUCCESS

It's time to have another look at our definitions of failure and success. What did you come up with after chapter three? How does your definition line up with those around you? If you haven't talked with your team, your close friends or your family about how they define success and failure – now's as good a time as any (after you've finished reading this chapter – of course!).

What does it look like for your vision to be a success? What are the milestones along the way? If we can't articulate what success for our vision looks like, how can we know if we need to make adjustments as we go? We need to look at our 'why', 'what', 'who' and 'how' regularly and be honest with one another about where we are fulfilling the vision as well as where we need to recalibrate.

As a leader, it's part of being accountable to your team for the vision and mission. It's about being transparent and vulnerable with your staff and identifying where things have gone awry as well as celebrating the aspects that are fulfilling the overall vision.

REFIRING AND RESTARTING

With that thought in mind, I'm just going to say it; sometimes businesses fail. With the best will in the world, a great plan, and stellar people – companies fall. With fifty per cent of small enterprises folding within the first five years and up to seventy per cent in the first decade – I know I'm speaking to a bunch of people who have tasted the bitterness of a business venture that soured.

Some of you need to hear this; failure is not the end. For many, this is not news – but the sting is still there. I understand, but it's not the end, just the end of the beginning. I've experienced failures, great and small, throughout my personal and business life, and I'm still here! I failed Jane as a husband, and our marriage almost didn't survive. It took a deliberate decision from both Jane and me – over and over – to work it out. We now have a fantastic marriage, but it has required effort, patience and a change in perspective, for me in particular.

I've had businesses that failed, both before and after Network Neighborhood. I've invested in companies that have gone horribly wrong. Would I start another business? Absolutely. Failure is not final. It's an opportunity to learn and apply it. A friend of mine who is a gifted scientist and inventor lost everything in a company collapse a few years back. That included houses, cars – every trapping and all the evidence of financial success. He could (and many would) have given up on his dreams and gone to work for somebody else. He hasn't. Instead, he's been humble, teachable and learned from the experience. He's back inventing and creating new businesses. His latest ventures look very different from his previous company – failure has proven to be an opportunity to do things in a new way – and it's working for him!

Life is not always fair, and brilliant ideas don't inevitably lead to successful outcomes. The disappointment, let alone the financial realities of business failure, can be the most bitter of pills to swallow. I'm generalising here, but I've noticed that in my own country of Australia, the emotional, mental and financial toll is often higher than somewhere like the U.S. There is an entrepreneurial spirit in America that instinctively views failure as a setback rather than a nail in the coffin. The notion of re-firing and re-starting appears ingrained in the American psyche.

In Australia, the idea of re-firing and restarting has traditionally carried a stigma. I think that in part, it's because Australians invest personally and financially so heavily in starting up a business. We are more likely to use our houses as capital, which means that a business failure tears at the fabric of every aspect of life. It differs from what I've seen in the U.S. where start-ups often rely on investor capital, making refiring and restarting a more natural proposition.

Another challenge faced by business owners in Australia, in particular, is the 'tall poppy' syndrome. It's a crazy scenario in which we want others to succeed, but only to the level that we are successful. If individuals or businesses experience success or favour that exceeds an 'acceptable' level in the eye of the beholder, they feel at liberty to take them down a peg or two, to wish it upon them, or to withhold support rather than champion them. In my opinion, it's been used effectively by the enemy to attack those with an entrepreneurial spirit.

While it is slowly changing in Australia, there is still an underlying unwillingness or inability to fully celebrate those who are successful or receive favour. This is by no means limited to the market place. It's infiltrated every pocket of society, including the church.

I saw it play out a couple of years ago with a pastor who has become a good friend. Jane and I were heading over to live in the U.S. for a season, and I decided to give the keys to my Aston Martin to this particular pastor so that he could enjoy driving it in our absence. He was initially hesitant as he didn't really know us, so checked with my pastor and mentor, Pete McHugh, who assured him, "That's Hugh. That's what he does."

A little while later, he drove the Aston to a state-wide pastors' meeting. He came back out to the car at the end of the day to find a note under the windscreen wiper. In it, the writer made some assumptions (never a good idea) and took my friend to task on having the audacity to drive such a car, suggesting that it didn't set the right example. My friend was understandably a bit upset, and I asked if I could respond.

I wrote a letter and explained that the use of the car was my gift to a friend and that for this person to act in such a manner, stole it not only from him but also from me as the giver. Favour and success are gifts, and when we denigrate them by ascribing to the 'tall poppy' view of others, we steal that gift.

I have another friend, a prosperous entrepreneur, who updated his car with an identical make and model so as not to draw attention to his success. The 'tall poppy' syndrome shames people and sends them into hiding. We are all the lesser for it. I believe that the only way to combat the 'tall poppy' syndrome is to transform the culture from one of competing to that of completing and learning how to celebrate the success of others.

A NEW PERSPECTIVE

Perspective is everything! We need to make sure that our view of life and business comes from the right angle. Greed, fear and corruption darken our lenses and narrow our world view. When we choose to see both failure and success through the eyes of God – they take on very different hues.

Thomas Edison 'failed' one thousand times before he created a working light bulb. When asked by a reporter, "How did it feel to fail one thousand times?" Edison replied, "I didn't fail one thousand times. The light bulb was an invention with one thousand steps" (They Did Not Fail, 2018).

What if your 'failure' is a stepping stone? What if there are lessons that you can learn and apply that will launch you into a new venture? Of course, there are also those times when we find ourselves in a Groundhog Day scenario; repeating the same failure, going around the same mountain. I know that mountain only too well.

While I chose not to deal with my anger issues, I found myself going around and around the same mountain. God wanted me to deal with my stuff, and I didn't want to. So, He kept poking me. Pete McHugh had a new book out, *You and the Creative Force of Frustration*; I'd given five hundred copies away and bought one hundred for myself – and ripped many to shreds. I couldn't get past the first chapter as he asked, "Do you ever find you are going around a mountain and ending up at the same spot?" (McHugh, 2002). Cue destroying the current copy!

The only way to stop making the same mistakes is to learn from them and do something different. I moved on once I got real about my stuff and let God heal me. God loves us too much to let us move to the next level before dealing with our issues at the current level. Maybe He needs you to address character issues, behavioural traits or relationship deficits so that you will flourish in the next season. My advice: let Him have his way, embrace the process and choose change. I promise it will be worth it.

If we choose to view both 'failure' and 'success' as opportunities to learn and grow, they become an entry point to new territory. I'm convinced that if the fruit of the Spirit is our compass, we will navigate the transition from the culture of pride to righteousness and generosity for all in the healthiest way possible.

> But the fruit produced by the Holy Spirit within you is divine love in all its varied expressions: joy that overflows, peace that subdues, patience that endures, kindness in action, a life full of virtue, faith that prevails, gentleness of heart, and strength of spirit. Never set the law above these qualities, for they are meant to be limitless. Galatians 5:22-23 The Passion Translation (TPT)

If we approach the transformation of ourselves and the business culture in this spirit, we will value people over profit and delight in calling the gold out in our teams. Failure and success won't define our worth, and our value for tasks will always be in submission to our desire to be in relationship with others. Given that most of us in the west spend a third of our lives at work, this can only have a positive benefit for our physical, mental, emotional and spiritual wellbeing.

WHEN IT ALL HITS THE FAN

OK, so you've put your heart and soul into making the transition from a culture of fear to favour, and suddenly there's resistance. More than that, it looks like things are falling apart; relationships strain, there are more misunderstandings than you can poke a stick at, the attack is coming from all sides. It's all part of the process, and you can make it. In fact, the pressure can be the making of both you and your business as you engage with your staff and work through this time.

And you know what, sometimes we make dumb decisions and have to deal with the consequences! We make bad choices because we are human. God is in the business of restoration, but he has also blessed us with free will, and there will be times when we have to face the natural consequences of our unwise choices.

King Solomon was the second child of King David and Bathsheba, the woman with whom King David had an affair and whose husband he had murdered. Solomon is known as the wisest king that has ever lived, and yet he made some terrible decisions! He introduced the nation of Israel to the worship of the pagan gods of his seven hundred wives and three hundred concubines, reaping the bitter harvest of a country divided and spiritually and morally compromised. The lack of wisdom in his personal life led to the oppression of his people and the division and ultimate destruction of the nation that had prospered under his father.

Solomon's story is a reminder that we can't compartmentalise our lives. We may fool ourselves into believing that our personal issues are separate from our business lives, but it's an illusion. My feelings of unworthiness manifested as anger issues and affected every part of my life. Don't make the mistake of thinking your stuff affects you alone.

God loves us and wants to work with us, knowing full well that we are human and will inevitably fail Him. It doesn't give Him pause for thought. He joyfully invites us to co-labour with Him and works with us in our frailties. What does this require of us? Humility, vulnerability, transparency, accountability and a willingness to change.

Jesus is the master at restoring people and launching them into callings that outstrip anything they had imagined for their lives. Jesus' restoration of Peter by the shores of Lake Galilee in John 21:15-19 (see chapter five) and Peter's subsequent role as the of the head of the church in Jerusalem is one of the more stunning examples of God's willingness to redeem, restore and relaunch.

If perfect God is not just willing but excited to work with us – what does that mean for us as leaders? I think it means that we don't throw people under the bus for their mistakes. We work with them to restore them and to find a solution that works for the business. If we require others to be perfect, we'd better be perfect ourselves. My experience tells me that when we extend grace – we not only create loyalty – we free people to soar.

DON'T WORRY, YOU WILL MAKE MISTAKES

Mistakes are an inevitable part of transforming the culture. I know, I've made many and I'm still learning. What keeps me going is the evidence I see of companies flourishing, with low staff turnover, leadership promoting others and a culture of completing rather than competing. The key is not in not making mistakes. The key is admitting when mistakes have been made, apologising where necessary, and making changes. It's time to flip the culture of blame and shame on its head. I've found that it produces an atmosphere in which people;

- Are more likely to admit to and own their mistakes.

- Are open to learning from their mistakes.

- Are willing to think in a fashion that is entirely outside the box, contributing to resolutions because they aren't simply part of the problem, they are part of the solution.

As leaders, it's imperative that we are transparent and accountable enough to admit when we've made mistakes, in both our personal and business world. I can't stress it enough; we can't expect others to own their mistakes if we aren't willing to change.

I learned this lesson painfully at Network Neighborhood when I oversaw the introduction of individual KPIs and employed managers who managed people rather than processes. The shift in atmosphere and culture was fast and quite devastating. Once I recognised my mistake, I had to humble myself and apologise to the staff for allowing it to happen. Then I had to follow my words up with action. We must be willing to make amends where necessary.

That meant making difficult decisions around staffing. We had to let go of some of the very people I'd brought in to do the managing! The sobering reality of what happened at Network Neighborhood was that the shift in culture, atmosphere and even structurally was not easily undone. Damage caused in a moment took far longer to rectify.

I tell you this to save you from making the same mistake. When we pioneer a new way, the pressure will come to revert to the status quo. People aren't malicious in their intent, and they don't want you to fail. It's just that when you have a toxic culture permeating every level of business, it's tough to shift. Even if people recognise the need for change, it is often a case of 'better the devil you know' (pun intended!). The people who counselled me to bring in more levels of management wanted the best for the company, and this was the way they had been taught to get there.

So, what will help you and your staff stay the course? I believe it's knowing and being sold on your 'why', 'what', 'how' and 'who'. If you can't articulate your vision and mission, you'll be like a rudderless ship at the mercy of the most powerful current and prevailing winds.

On a purely practical level, I've been asked on numerous occasions, "What should we do first; create a new vision or change the culture?" For me, it's always the vision. It's much easier to lead a team and influence the culture when you're working towards a shared vision. That way, you'll be able to transform the culture in line with the vision and mission. It works not only for businesses but for churches, sporting clubs or community groups – anywhere people come together.

If you've got a strong leader casting a vision that has been developed and refined with a team who have caught it, cultural change that serves the vision makes sense. Some will say that you need to change the culture before discovering your 'why' and 'what'. I think that unless you know where you are heading and what you are aiming for, it's going to be arduous work and you will find yourself chasing your tail.

FIXING THE MESS

I've said it over and over, and it bears repeating. In the end, life is about the quality of our relationships. Finances come and go, and the trappings of financial success are easily lost. If these things are the measure of our success – our wellbeing and that of our staff and families will be at the mercy of a merciless world system.

The best advice I can give you for when everything hits the fan – and it will – is SEEK HELP EARLY. Go and speak with trusted people. Seek counsel from those who've gone before you, and if you need to pay for it – then pay for it. When the voices tell you that you can't afford to pay for advice – ignore them. You may think you have no money now, but if you refuse to invest in the process of fixing the mess, you'll be much worse off.

Get somebody in to walk alongside you, to give another perspective and help you make the necessary changes. Pride tells us to go it alone. Greed, fear and corruption tell us that we have to go it alone. The truth is that we can only go so far on our own and that it's way better to walk in relationship with wise counsellors and advisors who will help make us and our business better.

A NEW LEADERSHIP PARADIGM FOR A NEW SEASON

So, what happens when you take the time to seriously address the purpose, vision and mission of your company? How do you lead authentically, look after the welfare of your staff, create success plans for your team, clients, and suppliers within the existing framework? As I said at the start of the chapter, trying to impose a new structure on an old one without addressing the fundamental cultural shifts leaves you open to the whole thing collapsing like a house of cards.

You may say, "But my company is small in comparison with others. What can I accomplish? Shouldn't we be looking to the multi-national, global businesses to lead the way?"

I agree that the challenge of changing the culture of a society can be overwhelming, so let's break it down. While ultimately, we are looking to affect society – we can immediately benefit our teams, their families and our communities. We bring this revolution from the ground up – not the top down!

The bottom line is – it can be tricky! If you're a new start-up or a small business, you are in the prime position to create a framework that embraces all the elements we've been discussing. If you are leading an established company – patience and perseverance need to be your friends!

Not only are you dealing with a framework and a system of doing business that is opposed to caring, sharing, and prosperity for all; you are working with people who have learnt to function within a system that seeks to divide and conquer. It begins with an education system developed for the industrial revolution that encourages conformity and rewards competition – but within incredibly narrow parameters and to the exclusion of a large slice of the population.

CREATING SAFETY FOR YOUR TEAM

I know I sound like a stuck record, but it's all about relationships. It's about going on a journey with your staff, clients, suppliers, family and friends. People need a reason to invest and stay invested in the vision and mission – so vulnerability, transparency and accountability on your part are crucial. Be upfront and honest about what you are trying to achieve and why. This will go a long way to creating a sense of safety for your team.

A crucial ingredient in creating safety as you transition is trust. Without trust, there is no safety. This was probably the hardest aspect of rebuilding the culture at Network Neighborhood. We had broken faith with the staff. It was as simple as that. If they were ever going to trust the others in leadership or me again, we had to give them a reason to do so. After the apologies, it was about inviting staff into the process of rebuilding the culture and making sure we followed up our words with action.

Integrity, honesty and accountability are crucial to the success of the process. At Network Neighborhood, we discovered that a policy on gossip was fundamental to transforming the culture.

> Your words are so powerful that they will kill or give
> life, and the talkative person will reap the consequences.
> Proverbs 18:21 The Passion Translation (TPT)

The first thing we did was identify what gossip is and what it looks like. My take on it is that if you are talking about somebody and you are not part of the situation or the solution – that's gossip. If you are a part of the situation or the answer but the other person is not – that's gossip. Just because you have the information, that doesn't give you the right to talk about it. We made it clear that there was no place for that in our company.

We must decide to believe the best of our people and call the gold out in them because the relationships we develop and the conversations we have are paramount. Remember, our job is to look after the welfare and wellbeing of our staff. The role of the team is to look after the business.

Communication will make or break the process. There will always be misunderstandings and mistakes while undergoing such a major cultural shift, and how we handle missteps and errors will set the tone for the whole process. When we call the gold out in people, accountability is one thing, accusation is entirely another. Even as we transitioned to a new culture, my natural inclination was to value task over people. I tended to shoot first and ask questions later, if at all. What I learned over time was to take a deep breath, step back and respond out of the relationship.

In the case of the employee who missed a deadline, it looks like, "Hey Mark, it's come to my attention that the deadline for this piece of work wasn't met. That's unusual for you. What's going on in your world? How can we work together as a team to help you?"

This approach only works if it's not lip service, and I'm consistent in my response to these types of situations. There's accountability, valuing the person, their life and our relationship (assuming this is true of Mark and not a pattern of behaviour), and making them part of the solution. When we come at challenges from a place of our relationship, when they know I am genuinely concerned for their welfare, and I know they have the best interests of the company at heart – these situations become opportunities for growth and an upgrade in our relationship.

This is leadership as opposed to managing. Tasks and processes are the only things that should be managed. People who are managed seldom feel valued or valuable, and if they believe they will be thrown under the bus; loyalty will go out the window pretty quickly!

THE PRICE OF SUCCESS

We've talked at length about flipping our definitions of both failure and success, for us, for our business and our employees. So what happens when we find ourselves caught out by our success? What happens when demand outstrips our ability to supply, and we find ourselves in the middle of a cashflow crisis?

It's one of the tightest spots that companies find themselves in and if not navigated well, can spell the end of an otherwise successful business. I propose that the wisdom of God is available to you. That there is an answer to your problem and that it probably lies in your continued commitment to unlocking and unleashing your team.

I remember when we faced this at Network Neighborhood, and it was quite terrifying! It was in 2008-09, as the world stared down the barrel of the GFC. In Australia, the federal government released cash across the board to stimulate the economy in hopes of fending off recession. We were in uncertain times and uncharted territory.

The major challenge associated with the cash stimulus was that schools now had the promise of funds. Many wisely decided to invest in technology and infrastructure. We'd built solid relationships with our network of school clusters, who now elected to purchase computers through us. Overnight we found ourselves receiving a million dollars in orders in a single day!

Of course, we didn't have the money to pay for all of these computers. We went to our suppliers who wanted payment up front while the schools were to pay us on delivery! It felt like an impossible situation for which we desperately needed a solution.

As a business, we were about creating success for us, our clients and as far as we could, our suppliers. That meant we kept short accounts and paid on time (or as close to as possible). We'd spent the preceding five years building those relationships, and now we needed their help. So we went back to them and said, "We have all these orders coming in, and they are guaranteed. We don't have the money to pay you, but the money for these computers is coming from the government – how can we work together?"

Our suppliers got back to us, "OK if you can show us the purchase orders on government letterhead, we will fund it, ship it and even deliver it. When the government money comes in, you pass it on to us."

Once we had picked our jaws up off the floor at the incredible favour we had been shown – we went about making it happen.

We set up a buying panel for schools so that everyone got a fair deal in the spirit of righteousness and generosity. Why should a small school not be able to buy at the same price as a big school? So, we set up a standard computer for the beginner, intermediate and advanced levels. People were able to personalise the specifications for their device – but it started with a level playing field. Everyone knew the price, there were no backdoor deals, and the schools loved it.

We then set up an online ordering portal for schools so that they could log in and do it all themselves. Computers were drop shipped to the student's homes pre-imaged, set up, and ready to use.

Our cash flow 'crisis' ended up being one of the best things that could have happened! When you flip the culture in and around your business from that of greed, fear and corruption to one of a caring, sharing and prosperity for all, everything works together for good. We developed an entirely new streamlined process for school communities that ensured every student had a personalised device that connected to a network. This was the fulfilment of the original vision God gave me, and He used our crisis to achieve it!

We need to be willing to have our mindsets challenged and changed. Good businesses go to the wall because we've bought the line about the way that things are. We need to allow creative solutions to flow. When we value human capital before financial capital, we will find that economics takes care of itself. When we value money before people – the struggle may well get the best of us.

LEADERSHIP THAT TRANSFORMS

My good friend, Ford Taylor, has been on this journey with numerous businesses. The story of our meeting and subsequent working partnership is another God set up that I'll share about more fully in chapter seven. For now, the nutshell version is that while my team and I were building and running Network Neighborhood with a culture of generosity, Ford was doing the same thing on the other side of the world. Ford has gone on to develop the Transformational Leadership (TL) (FSH Strategy Consultants, 2018) program and has helped thousands of businesses, organisations and even cities transform their culture by training leaders to have a positive impact wherever they have influence.

He has developed, documented and teaches five stages of the leadership journey that dovetail beautifully with a generous culture of caring and shared prosperity. We won't be going into great detail for now, but I want to give you some of the language that Ford uses as I think it's incredibly helpful.

The first stage involves "vision" or visionary leadership. It's when you as a leader cast vision for the 'why' and 'what' of your company and the culture within which it's embedded.

Stage two is the "cohesive" phase. It's about serving and teaching – taking on the role of servant-leader, modelling generosity and teaching others how to walk in a new way.

The third stage of leadership is about giving "functional responsibility" to people as you train and equip them. It's about creating a safe place for people to grow and develop. It's about valuing what others bring to the table, calling out the gold and providing opportunities for your team to contribute to the 'why', 'what', 'how' and 'who'.

I recommend that you develop success plans for individual team members at this stage. There's no better time to have people considering their 'why', 'what', 'how' and 'who' than in conjunction with the business. We are creating success for all, our business, staff, clients and the wider community. Get them thinking about how they can contribute beyond themselves personally as well as how the business can help bring about societal change. It's an exciting time if you look at it from the perspective of setting everyone up for success.

Ford calls stage four "Relactional" and no, it's not a typo! This concept is pure gold with the potential to set people free in amazing measure. Let me explain. "Relactional" is the bringing together of two styles of leadership at either end of a continuum. With highly 'relational' leaders on one end, and highly 'transactional' leaders on the other. It's pretty self-explanatory, 'relational' leaders are all about building relationships before completing tasks. At the other end, 'transactional' leaders are all about completing tasks or transactions before building relationships. In the end, neither extreme is particularly helpful.

For a long time, I was a transactional leader focussed on tasks over people, and it led to a bunch of damaged relationships. On the other hand, when leaders focus on connections to the exclusion of the transactions, not a lot gets accomplished. The goal for leaders is to combine the relational and transactional to become more "relational". It's about valuing people over profits while honouring the business of doing business. You'll find that as you recognise those traits in your team and encourage them to honour one another, the result is a more cohesive unit that acknowledges people for the strengths they bring to the table.

As Ford says,

> *"Many leaders have been taught how to manage people, yet may not have been given the practical tools to lead people and manage the processes around them. By removing personal and process constraints, individuals can develop into the kind of leader they aspire to become and foster the kind of organization they aspire to lead."* (The FSH Group, 2013)

It's all about equipping and empowering people to bring their whole selves and unique identities to the process. There is unity in diversity, and we need both relational and transactional people in our organisations to bring balance. Once people understand their tendency and how others on the team relate, it opens the door to a constructive dialogue.

The fifth and final stage is "continuous improvement". It's characterised by "letting go" or empowering, as well as "evaluating". When you create a culture of trust, safety, integrity and accountability, continuous improvement doesn't inspire dread in your staff. It becomes an opportunity to revisit your collective and individual 'why', 'what', 'how' and 'who' regularly. I would suggest that when it comes to the vision and mission of your company, a yearly review would be the minimum requirement to ensure that your mission is accomplishing the vision. For individuals, we did six-monthly reviews of their success plans. It's easier to make small corrections to your course than it is to turn the ship around as it hits land!

THE BOTTOM LINE

You can ride the wave and not only survive; you can flourish! A lot of what we've talked about comes down to a change in perspective and mindset. If you remain humble, accountable and teachable, there is really nothing that can ultimately take you down. When you help instil these values in your team, not just giving them lip service, but living them out transparently – you will have a bunch of solution-focussed people who have your back!

Navigating the highs and lows of business is about how we value and develop our relationships with others. As I said earlier, the divide between personal and business is an illusion. One always affects the other. It's not that we need to have it all together in both, but rather, that we own our stuff and commit to dealing with it.

There are many ways that you, as a leader, can help the process.

As I mentioned in chapter three, getting a mentor has been a crucial ingredient in my leadership journey – somebody who could speak into my life. I actively sought the wisdom and insight of a person who loves me enough to hold up a mirror, allowing me to see how my words and actions affect others.

We all need those who will hold us to account and have permission to speak frankly into our worlds. In my case, I tend towards sarcasm in my humour, and at times, I have said things in jest that have pulverised people. Had my mentor Pete, along with Jane, and dear friends not loved me enough to bring correction, I may still be clueless about how my words were received.

You need to be able to articulate what both success and failure look like for you. Develop your definitions in the context of your most intimate relationships. If you have determined that success looks like you putting in eighty hours a week and that's what you are doing – that's ok. However, if your definition of success is that you arrive home at a reasonable hour and spend time with the family and you are working an eighty-hour week – that's going to be a problem. It's the quickest way to bring guilt and shame into the equation.

It may also be that your expectations are based on an ideal rather than the reality of being in business. This is where I think the counsel of trusted advisors is invaluable. Choose wisely. Look for those who have gone before you and blazed a trail! Just because someone is a 'business advisor' doesn't mean they are right for your business, particularly when you are challenging a toxic business culture. If they don't understand what you are trying to achieve – they won't be right for your business. We can only take people to the places we have been ourselves. Those who only know the culture of greed, fear and corruption can't help lead you into one based on caring, sharing and prosperity for all.

And beyond all of that, I encourage you not to forget the world outside of your immediate sphere of influence. Saying that we will be generous once we have transitioned doesn't cut it for me. If you want a culture of generosity to thrive – be generous. If you want a culture of kindness – be kind. We can't expect them to appear magically at the end of the process. We must weave them into everything we do – they need to be part of our authentic expression. If they aren't currently – my advice is to seek God on his heart. I had no interest in social justice until I said "Yes" to God and went on a business trip with Pete McHugh to Cambodia, where my heart changed in a moment.

ACTION STEPS

Take some time to sit with these questions and answer them honestly. You may need to bring others in on the conversation – it will be worth it!

1. Can you articulate success and failure for yourself and your business?

2. Are your expectations based on the ideal or the reality of living and doing business?

3. Where do you sit on the leadership continuum?

4. Are you more relational?

5. Do you tend towards the transactional?

6. What steps can you take towards becoming a 'relactional' leader? If you aren't sure, why not ask others on your leadership team – or if you are feeling brave – ask your team!

7. Is your business a place of safety for your staff? Do they feel valued as people and for what they contribute to the organisation?

8. How have your thoughts progressed on finding a mentor and seeking out trusted advisors for your business?

You can find out more about Ford Taylor and TL by visiting https://transformlead.com/our-team/ford-taylor/

In the next chapter, we get to what it's all about – it's a big world out there, and it needs you.

CHAPTER SEVEN

There's a whole world waiting!

I admit it; I'm excited about this chapter. You're going to see a few exclamation marks because it's my passion, my purpose, my vision and mission to see you released to make a difference in the lives of people you may never meet. You can change the world through the way you conduct your life and business.

Everything we have talked about is leading up to this moment. It's a big world out there, and it needs you! We don't live in a vacuum, and we certainly don't run our organisations in isolation. Being in business means that we are blessed with the opportunity to make a difference in the lives of others in our families, businesses, communities, nations and beyond.

For a long time, I thought that being in business was all about me. It was about proving myself to the world and accumulating the trappings of 'success' as dictated by society. It was as I chose to seek God's wisdom in the context of a relationship with Him that things began to change.

The success of our business ventures, in particular, Network Neighborhood, are the direct result of surrendering to God and

His plans. He is the ultimate multi-tasker. He used the success of NN to undo me, rip up my foundations and lay new ones! He has been rebuilding me ever since, exposing the lies I believed and renewing my mind.

He has been changing my perspective, slowly but surely. I am by no means a finished work – as anyone who knows me will attest. But I have made it my mission to say "Yes" to God, and I've found that it is the only way I want to live. That's because it's a choice. Every day we can choose to say yes to His plans, but we are also at liberty to say "No, not today". That's the beauty of life in God. He has a purpose and plan for our lives that is bigger than anything we can imagine, and probably vastly different to the one we envisage, BUT He will not force us to participate. Free will is something that He does not violate because to do so would violate His nature.

In the words of Jesus in Revelation,

> Behold, I'm standing at the door, knocking. If your heart is open to hear my voice and you open the door within, I will come in to you and feast with you, and you will feast with me. Revelation 3:20 The Passion Translation (TPT)

I can't encourage you strongly enough – open the door! The feast He offers is more significant than any trial you will encounter along the way. Jesus promised that He came to give us life in abundance.

> I am the Gateway. To enter through me is to experience life, freedom, and satisfaction. A thief has only one thing in mind – he wants to steal, slaughter, and destroy. But I have come to give you everything in abundance, more than you expect – life in its fullness until you overflow! John 10:9-10 The Passion Translation (TPT)

It's a two-way exchange. We let Him in by opening the door and at the same time, we enter in via the Gateway – Jesus. After all, this is a relationship!

I've said before that at times I find it hard to recount the story of Network Neighborhood because it feels like my part has been to say "Yes" to God and then watch Him do it all. All He asks of any of us is that we say, "Yes Lord" and trust Him to lead us in the process.

I'm excited to share this part of the journey with you. I want to inspire you with what is possible when we let go and let God order our steps. I won't lie; when you are used to being in control and operating within the culture of greed, fear and corruption, it feels utterly counter-intuitive to do some of the things He asks.

God is inviting us into a kingdom culture – one grounded in generosity and righteousness that values people over profit. We've been living in a construct designed by us (ably assisted by the enemy) and placed over the top of the kingdom culture. It's time to unplug from The Matrix!

So, let's get into this and start dreaming with God!

THE SOCIAL CONSCIENCE OF BUSINESS

Have you noticed the change? Have you noticed a shift in the social conscience of companies on a global scale? God is on the move and those with ears to hear and eyes to see are picking up on the principles that God has woven into the fabric of the universe. They may not all know Him yet, but they understand the law of sowing and reaping.

It turns out that the "greed is good" speech of Gordon Gekko in *Wall Street* is a load of rubbish. Greed and its nasty bedfellows fear and corruption breed more greed, fear and corruption and are divisive by nature. It is a simple and universal truth that a house divided will not stand, so this particular house of cards must fall.

When we combine kingdom principles with our 'why', 'what', 'who' and 'how' everybody reaps the benefits. The Chan Zuckerberg Initiative (CZI) is a great example. The vision for the philanthropic investment company founded by Priscilla Chan and Mark Zuckerberg is "A Future for Everyone." Their 'what' is "to find new ways to leverage technology, community-driven solutions, and collaboration to accelerate progress in Science, Education, and within our Justice and Opportunity work" (CZI, 2019). Their 'who' is organisations that are working towards these goals, and their 'how' is wisely funding those who do the research, develop cures, dream of new methods for educating our children and so on.

It's about legacy. It's about leaving the world a better place for having us in it, and it's how I want to live.

STEWARDING OUR RESOURCES

What is in your hand right now? What are you stewarding? If you have a relationship with God, what has He given you and who has He put on your heart?

Jesus had a lot to say about the way that we manage the finances entrusted to us. In His parable on financial stewardship – a wealthy man gives his servants money while he leaves on business. On his return, he rewards those who stewarded the funds well, making money with the money. But for the one who was afraid and did nothing, he was harsh.

> "Angered by what he heard, the master said to him, 'You're an untrustworthy and lazy servant! If you knew I was a shrewd

and ruthless businessman who always makes a profit, why didn't you deposit my money in the bank? Then I would have received it all back with interest when I returned. But because you were unfaithful, I will take the one thousand gold coins and give them to the one who has ten thousand. For the one who has will be given more, until he overflows with abundance. And the one with hardly anything, even what little he has will be taken from him.' Matthew 25:26-29 The Passion Translation (TPT)

When we are faithful with the little we have, God can trust us with more because we're not hoarding it for ourselves – we understand that money is a means to an end. When God gives us the vision – we can be sure that He will supply the finances. What we'll require is an upgrade of faith because more often than not, the natural circumstances will fly in the face of the vision!

Success in business, favour and blessing, are never just about us. Looking after our families is important, but we can't divorce ourselves from the rest of the world. God even says that caring for the welfare of others is to know Him. I want to know Him!

He defended the cause of the poor and needy, and so all went well. Is that not what it means to know me?" declares the Lord. Jeremiah 22:16 (NIV)

EXPECT THE UNEXPECTED: CAMBODIA

If there's one thing I've learned over the years about life in God, it's that He doesn't wait until we have our lives sorted before asking us to step up. Time and time again, I've experienced the call of God while working through my issues or experiencing challenges within my business. I've witnessed the same thing with many of my friends.

Seriously, while I never want to put God in a box, He seems to consistently have far greater belief in our abilities than we do. When He knows that our heart's response to Him is "Yes", and we put our money where our faith is – regardless of what is going on in our lives – He trusts us with greater mysteries and asks us to participate and co-create in ways we could never have imagined.

For Jane and me, Cambodia is of those moments. If you could have seen the challenges swirling around us and the business, it certainly didn't *look* like the right time to introduce a whole new calling. Probably a good thing we aren't God!

I'm reminded of the words of the apostle Paul;

> "We are like common clay jars that carry this glorious treasure within, so that the extraordinary overflow of the power will be seen as God's, not ours. Though we experience every kind of pressure, we're not crushed. At times we don't know what to do, but quitting is not an option." 2 Corinthians 4:7-8
> The Passion Translation (TPT)

It was soon after buying out my business partner at NN. I was trying to do everything in the business and became impossible to live with – literally. God allowed the pressure to expose my insecurities and unhealthy coping mechanisms. My inability to let others in culminated in me moving out of our family home on Christmas Eve, 2007. Jane was instrumental in helping me appreciate the toll my inner turmoil was taking on those I loved, damaging our relationships. One of the qualities I admire in her is that she is a peacemaker, not a peacekeeper. She is one who seeks to bring peace but isn't afraid to confront issues in a manner that disarms.

I'm not so gentle in my dealings. I tend to charge in and say, "Look, here's the issue people. We don't have to look for the elephant in the room; it's sitting right there! Should we address this right now or are we going to dance around this thing?"

Confronting an issue isn't bad; unresolved conflict is a killer. I think that's why God allowed me to come face to face with my dysfunctional behaviour in what felt like a fairly dramatic fashion.

It was while I was living away from our family home that God started ordering Jane's steps in a way that ultimately changed the direction of our lives and continues to send us on the most incredible adventures!

I've asked Jane to tell her part of the story because it's hers to recount, not mine.

IN HER OWN WORDS

Hugh was staying with friends when God challenged me to step out. Our church was and still is involved in Cambodia. I knew that short-term missions' teams were travelling over but knew very little else about it. So I was a bit surprised, to say the least, when God told me to go to Cambodia.

Honestly, I ignored it for a little bit. Then God repeated the call, "You need to go to Cambodia." I thought, well ok then. I've learnt not to dilly-dally too much when He's insistent!

A couple from church, John and Pauline O'Connell, headed up short-term trips with a focus on social justice. That Sunday they gave an update about the team preparing to leave for Cambodia in two weeks. God spoke again, "That's the one. That's the trip you are to go on."

I was shocked, "Ah, God, no. There's no way I can do that. They've got everything organised!"

"Just ask them," came the reply.

Long story short...two weeks later, I headed off with the team to Cambodia with no idea why I was going.

It was an eye-opening experience. We visited people our church was supporting and travelled out to rural areas, distributing medicines and the like. We took time out to visit the Tuol Sleng Genocide Museum and the Killing Fields, and while it was impacting and I felt drawn to the beautiful Cambodian people, I didn't feel a specific call to action from the Lord.

What I did hear loud and clear from God was, "Hugh needs to come to Cambodia."

I protested. "Seriously Lord, he doesn't want anything to do with social justice, and he certainly doesn't want to come to Cambodia. If you want him here, you tell him!"

I wasn't keen on His response, "No, it would be best if it comes from you."

Great, I get to be the messenger!

We returned home, and I delivered the message, "Hugh, God wants you to go to Cambodia." He wasn't overly convinced, but a short while later, Peter McHugh asked Hugh to travel with him to Cambodia on a four-day ministry trip. I'll let Hugh finish his part of the story a little later.

In the meantime, I was having my own conversation with the Lord. I remember saying, "OK, I've done what you asked me to do God. But why did you want me there? Surely it wasn't for me to go and just observe the suffering and poverty of the people?" He didn't answer straight away.

A week later, I was sitting at my hairdressers when my eye caught a *Women's Weekly* magazine. In big, bold font, it read "Child Trafficking in Cambodia" right there on the cover! The article was heart-wrenching and left me sobbing in my chair. Like so many, I had no idea about the modern-day slavery taking place across the globe.

Another week went by and Banning Liebscher from Bethel Church, Redding, spoke at church about the dreams God gives us. He told the story of a woman who had been given the dream to do something about ending human trafficking. She had no idea what to do but chose to say "Yes" to God.

So I said to God, "If this is something you want me involved in – I don't know how to do it, so you'll have to bring other women with a similar dream."

I told no one, but within a week, a friend gave me a book by Somaly Mam, a woman trafficked as a child in Cambodia. My friend had been directed by God to buy the book, read it and pass it along to me. I read it and gave it to my friend Lisa, who was also on the Cambodia trip.

All of this was within weeks of returning from Cambodia. Lisa and I were dreaming together about what we might do when Hugh came to me and said, "God's told me that you need to go back to Cambodia."

I agreed we needed to return at some stage, but Hugh had other ideas, "No, I mean you need to go back in the next couple of days."

"Ah no," I said, "we have nothing organised, no connections, no plan, nothing."

God had gone and done it again! I relented, "OK if you can get us flights, we'll go."

We reached out to the pastors of New Life Church, Jesse and Soar McCaul, whom we'd met on our previous trip, and they organised accommodation for us. Lisa and I attended New Life on Sunday and Jesse introduced us to people who offered to set up meetings for the following week. And just like that, God's plan unfolded.

One of our meetings was with Hagar International, an organisation dedicated to providing recovery services for survivors of human trafficking, slavery and abuse. One of its initiatives was a manufacturing plant that produced bags for export sale. While they had customers in Europe and the U.S., they hadn't yet been able to break into the Australian market. There was an obvious opportunity, but neither Lisa nor I were convinced that this was what the Lord was asking of us.

We ended our trip a few days early as a travel advisory to leave the country was issued in the lead up to the Cambodian general election. Lisa and I landed in Kuala Lumpur for a two-day stopover on our way home. On the first night, I had a dream. I dream, but ones like this are few and far between. I was asleep, but it felt like I was awake. God laid out what we were to do. Yes, we were to have a bag business importing bags from Cambodia, and we were to call it Stop-Start.

"What kind of name is that?" I asked God.

"It's not about the bags – it's about STOP the trafficking and START a new life," He replied.

So just like that, Stop-Start was born and grew. We worked with Hagar International, selling bags and raising awareness of the issues of trafficking and modern-day slavery.

IN HIS OWN WORDS

Here is where our stories intersect. As Jane said, when she first came to me with the word from God about going to Cambodia, I was thoroughly unconvinced. I felt no desire to go to Cambodia, and I wasn't interested in social justice issues. I was super busy, stressed, feeling responsible for the staff and with the financial burden weighing heavily. Combine that with our separation and me dealing with my issues – I wasn't in the most receptive frame of mind!

Jane had founded and was working with Stop-Start when Pete McHugh asked me to go with him to meet with church and business leaders in Cambodia. Nothing remarkable transpired on our trip except that I couldn't walk onto the Killing Fields. It was brutal, and spiritually I was incredibly affected.

It was as we were leaving that it happened. I saw a young boy. He wasn't begging, just standing there looking at me, his eyes like deep, dark holes. I asked God, "Well, what do you want me to do with that?" Then, for only the second time in my life, I heard the audible voice of God, "I want you to bring hope to the nations by helping people achieve their God-given potential."

I knew that there was only one possible response from me; I was all in. I came back and supported Jane and Stop-Start while continuing to work through my stuff and in the business.

It was a couple of years into our relationship with Hagar International and the manufacturing plant in Cambodia that we found out the board had decided to close the manufacturing plant. We were visiting the plant when we received the news. As we walked up to the building that day, Jane had a vision of a sign over the door that read STOP START. She initially thought she was hallucinating until the Lord said to me, "Why don't you buy the plant – you could help." I don't know anything about manufacturing – but sure, God!

We believed God wanted us to help, but the reality was that the plant, all of the manufacturing equipment and other machinery was worth over AUD $200,000. There was no way we could afford it. I put it to God, and He replied, "It's OK, you'll buy the plant with all the machinery for $5,000." I believe Him when He speaks – but this was pretty unbelievable!

God is true to His word, and the next day we got a call from the manager to ask if we'd like to buy the plant and all the machinery for the princely sum of $5,000!

That's how we became involved on a whole new level in Cambodia. We employed managers and sourced new markets for bags and other products. Women and girls, some rescued out of trafficking, and others with disabilities were trained in various aspects of production, including manufacturing and administration. It was a huge endeavour, and by far the biggest challenge was overseeing everything from Australia.

By 2012, the business was running well and producing quality items, but we felt that our involvement was coming to an end. We didn't want to close it down and very much wanted the women to have an investment in the company, so we travelled to Cambodia to find a solution. We'd been there for a week and were becoming increasingly frustrated. It seemed that no doors were opening, and every meeting resulted in another dead end.

On the last day of our visit, a friend's mother suggested that we contact a local pastor. She explained, "His name is Bora. He's a pastor, but he also has his own t-shirt company and is looking to expand."

We both felt the hand of the Lord on the connection, so called him and asked to meet. We got together, heard his story, told him the history of the plant and asked him if he was interested.

"Yes!" came his enthusiastic reply, "That sounds amazing. I'd love to get involved with something like that. The only problem is that I don't have any money."

We knew the answer to that one immediately. "That's OK. We don't want money; we want to gift it to you."

"What do you mean? You want to do what?" was the incredulous response as he started to cry.

"Well, we know that this is what God wants us to do and that the plant will be in good hands." So that's what we did. We had received a gift from God, and we passed it along at the right time to the right person.

In the words of Jesus,

> "Heal the sick, raise the dead, cleanse the lepers, cast out demons. Freely you received, freely give." Matthew 10:8 (NASB)

Bora has taken the business from strength to strength, diversifying along the way. They've secured a government contract making shirts and shorts for school students and the women have a stake in the company, changing the lives of their families and communities.

We say "Yes" to God. The vehicle He chooses is not ours; it is always His. The vision doesn't change, but sometimes the vehicle does. If we attach ourselves to the manifestation of the vision rather than the vision itself, we may miss the even bigger purpose and plan – to release others into their God-given vision – and us into our next adventure!

KINGDOMPRENEURS – IT'S A THING!

When I began in business, I didn't know Jesus. My business was about me, about proving my worth and yes, providing for my family – but primarily as evidence of my ability to do and have it all. I met Jesus and was now a Christian who ran a business. Tithing and giving became my new normal. I started a 'Christian business', experiencing the joys and challenges along the way. Then I started hearing the language of kingdom businesses and seeing a way that was about more than following Christian principles. It's about doing business God's way. It's about running enterprises His way, and funding initiatives as He directs.

There are people, business people, all around the world with stories to tell like ours. God is releasing a new breed of entrepreneurs who are kingdom minded. I was spending time with God the other day (while soaking in our hot tub), and He gave me this word;

> Kingdompreneur (N): a person who is creating and doing business God's way, for His purposes.

My prayer is that you become a Kingdompreneur who unleashes love on the world as directed by the King of the kingdom.

SIP IT FORWARD

God is fun! I have so much fun dreaming and doing with Him. One of the things I love about Him is the way He engineers 'coincidences' that leave you laughing, crying, and shaking your head at His magnificent ways and brilliant sense of humour!

I want to share one of these moments with you. I can imagine the angels watching on, waiting for me to make the discovery and having a good chuckle. I was in the Cambodian capital of Phnom

Penh for a series of meetings and happened to be walking past one of the many buildings when I looked up and saw the logo of my brother's winery, 'Mollydooker', emblazoned on the side.

Bemused, I rang my brother in South Australia,

"So, Sparky, I'm standing on this road in Phnom Penh, and I look up and see your logo…"

"Oh, you're outside our school," he said casually.

"What do you mean, your school?"

Sparky explained, "We've been funding some schools in Cambodia. It sounds like you're standing outside one of our new ones. Just go inside."

Unbeknownst to me, my brother and sister-in-law had also become involved in sowing into communities in Cambodia, using their business, Mollydooker Wines as the vehicle. As he explained it, they decided to finance their schools through a yearly fundraiser called 'Sip It Forward'.

Every year they produce a Merlot called 'Sip It Forward', at the Mollydooker Winery in McLaren Vale, South Australia. All of the proceeds from the sale of the wine go to supporting the schools. There are currently 4,000 children receiving an education through this simple, beautiful example of my brother and his family bringing what they have and impacting individuals, families, communities and the whole of society. The school program is called 'Transform Cambodia'!

It gets even better. As I walked inside the school in Phnom Penh, I heard a voice coming from the fourth floor calling my name, "Mr Hugh! Mr Hugh!"

"What?" I was puzzled as to who could be calling my name as until this moment I didn't even know my brother was working in

Cambodia. I looked up to see a familiar face hurtling down the stairs towards me.

"Mr Hugh!" shouted Ranika as he launched himself at me to wrap me in a joy-filled hug. I had to laugh and marvel. Ranika had been my translator in Cambodia for four years for the projects we were doing. He stopped working for me because he went to work for another organisation; turns out it was my brother's!

God is looking for Kingdompreneurs who see beyond themselves and expect to receive strategies for releasing resources to benefit others. When we submit our plans, as well as our human, social and financial capital to Him, He will show up in the most surprisingly creative and groundbreaking ways!

MAKING THE MAIN THING THE MAIN THING

There is a much-quoted African proverb, "If you want to go fast, go alone. If you want to go far, go together." In chapter one, I said that I believe the purpose of business is ultimately to prosper and provide for the welfare of the members of any society. When we are disconnected because we swallow the lie of the limited pie and winners and losers, we will leave a wasteland of damaged relationships and broken people in our wake.

Jesus' mission was to restore the relationship we lost when Adam and Eve decided to be like God rather than enjoy eternal oneness with Him.

> "I pray for them all to be joined together as one even as you and I, Father, are joined together as one. I pray for them to become one with us so that the world will recognise that you sent me. For the very glory you have given to me I have given them so that they will be joined together as one and experience the same unity that we enjoy.

You live fully in me and now I live fully in them so that they will experience perfect unity, and the world will be convinced that you have sent me, for they will see that you love each one of them with the same passionate love that you have for me."
John 17:21-23 The Passion Translation (TPT)

It's the main thing. Everything else is either adding to or taking away from the way we relate to God and our fellow human beings. When you choose to make the main thing the main thing, you will be surprised at how God links you with others carrying the same purpose, vision and mission.

In 2017 I was surprised by God yet again as He introduced me to a remarkable man who has not only carried His heart for transforming the culture of businesses but who has faithfully stewarded what God has put in his hands.

TRANSFORMATIONAL LEADERSHIP (TL)

The longer I live with God, the more I recognise that He is first and foremost interested in connecting people with Himself and each other. It's a comfort to know that He gives us others to walk alongside. I love that I have a piece of the puzzle, and others possess pieces that fit with mine. No part is more valuable than another – what's important is that we come together – recognising each other's value and joining our pieces to form the picture that God is creating.

The most important thing for me to do is to be who God created me to be and to do what he has for me to do. If I walk in authenticity with God and man, with all of my strengths and weaknesses, my triumphs and my failings, I will be open to partnering with others. I won't be caught up in ego or be jealous of those who own another piece of the puzzle; I'll want to work with them!

Before I get carried away, there is a reason for my ramblings! After all that God has walked Jane and me through, the lessons learned and the keys He has given us for changing the culture of business, we are now beginning to see the bigger picture. God is joining our piece of the puzzle with those of other people, and it blows me away!

When we sold Network Neighborhood in 2014, we had no idea what God had planned. Honestly, if I were God, I would have done it differently. NN represented a steady income that released us to work around the world to see our purpose, vision and mission come to fruition. When I pointed out the obvious benefits of keeping NN to Him and asked why I had to sell the business, I was surprised by His reply.

"Hugh, I'm selfish. I wanted all of you."

More recently, the Lord revealed that I have been in a season of preparation. For what? Only He has the inside running on that one, but eighteen months ago, He introduced me to a man carrying a substantial piece of the puzzle.

In September 2017, I was invited to attend the European Economic Summit in South Africa. I agreed to go, but Jane wasn't keen. I was travelling throughout Asia with our dear friend Leif Hetland, and it had been a pretty hectic trip. I was exhausted, but I felt God telling me to go. A couple of days before the summit, Jane decided to come, so I booked her flights, and she arrived in Johannesburg the day before me. I missed my original flight from Singapore and so was re-routed through Dubai and Cape Town before arriving in a more than slightly delirious state at three in the morning.

I made it through the first speaker but could barely keep my eyes open, and it was pretty uninspiring stuff. The next speaker announced was a guy called Ford Taylor to speak on transformational business leadership. I turned to Jane, "That's awesome. I'm going to get some sleep."

"Just stay", she said. "I was out for a walk yesterday, and I met Ford. We walked and talked for a while. I think you are going to get a lot out of what he has to say."

I was in no state to pay attention. "No honey, I'm wrecked. I'm not going to take in anything." But somehow, I found myself sitting there as he spoke.

Ford only had an hour and talked about leadership, the challenges of leadership and the challenges of leadership and faith. I heard a resounding YES in my spirit as he spoke. It was precisely how we'd tried to live, but I didn't have the language to explain it to others.

Everything he said was what we had done innately in our company without knowing why. We'd stumbled into it early on but had never named it. I had to meet Ford, so Jane introduced us, and the first thing I asked was how he had come across these principles. It turns out that he also stumbled into them without understanding what they were.

Ford found that when implemented, these principles revolutionised his businesses, causing them to thrive, so he began writing and teaching Transformational Leadership courses. As his companies flourished, he went to his pastor and asked, "By any chance is this stuff in the Bible?" His pastor's response was one of excitement, "Absolutely! You don't know what you've got your hands on; all of it is in the Bible!"

"Well, where is it?" Ford asked.

"You go and find out for yourself, Ford" was his pastor's reply.

Ford rose to the challenge, studied, and discovered the biblical principles attached to everything he was doing. He took his findings to three other pastors for their opinion. Unfortunately, that didn't go so well. As Ford tells the story, all three declared that his teaching was not from the Bible and that he was basically a heretic bringing false instruction.

Not what you would hope for! It was a twelve-month journey with those pastors, but eventually, all three came back, apologised and agreed that the principles were all in the Bible, confessing that they had no idea what to do with them!

The following day I received a cryptic text from Ford, *I had a dream last night, and God was speaking to me. What is He saying to you?*

All I knew was that I wanted to find out more. While the Transformational Leadership (TL) courses were available online, I wanted to see Ford in action and be part of a live event. We suggested that Jane and I could travel to wherever he was presenting. Ford was keen, so we organised to meet him in Cincinnati where he was part of a city-wide transformation event. From there we arranged to travel together and be a fly on the wall at a corporate training event.

In March 2018, we landed in the U.S. and attended three Transformational Leadership events in seven days. By the end of our time, I knew that I needed to work with Ford. Oh, and Ford told us that the word God had given him was that he and I needed to work together. Neither of us was sure what it looked like, but we were willing.

Ford has TL trainers around the world, so I also trained, and it felt like second nature. I completed the training in record time, and now we present together around the world. We were back in South Africa recently, and one of my friends commented to Ford, "If we didn't know that you had written the material, we would have sworn that Hugh wrote it!"

Both Ford and I understand that Transformational Leadership is an idea from God whose time has come. The moment has arrived for God's truths to be displayed and taught because they are the best way to do life and business.

Cincinnati has experienced a radical turnaround thanks to their adoption of the principles of Transformational Leadership that Ford has imparted over the last fifteen years. A few years ago now, the city and church elders signed what we call a 'social covenant.' This covenant declared that they would treat each other with respect, honesty and integrity. They agreed that they would not participate in gossip. They even took out the front pages of every newspaper in Cincinnati announcing how they were going to work together for the city and asking the citizens to hold them accountable.

What they've seen happen is miraculous! There has been an incredible reduction in the city's crime rate, along with a decrease in drug-related offences. The employment rates have increased along with the overall wealth of the city. People are treated with dignity and respect, even when they disagree. There has been a city-wide transformation stemming from the decision of those in leadership to embrace a relational way of leading.

THE BOTTOM LINE

Do you have your 'why', 'what', 'who' and 'how'? What's the legacy you want to leave future generations through your business? How will the community be better off because of your company?

How do you define success? For me, it went from making money to helping people tap into, develop and share their God-given potential. It's ultimately about building relationships with my teams, clients and suppliers that release them to soar if they choose. I don't always get it right – but that's part of the journey. I own my stuff, allow others to own theirs, and together we get on with the business of making a difference in the world. That's a reason to go to work every day!

When our businesses become a vehicle for transformation, they will cease to own us. When we are no longer captive to the culture of greed, fear and corruption, it's amazing how our eyes open to recognise the needs of others. When we agree with kingdom culture, we position ourselves to be of ultimate benefit to society.

That requires humility on our part. I know, back to that old chestnut. Remember Rick Warren's words,

"Humility is not thinking less of yourself; it's thinking of yourself less." (Warren, 2002)

What is it that's going to draw you and drive you? What is it that will keep you going in business through the tough times? What is it that's going to bring you through the great times and inspire you to help others? How are you going to make a difference in the lives of others?

ACTION STEPS

As we near the end of our journey, take some time to dream. Dream alone. Dream with others. Find out what inspires your staff. Get to know what your team are passionate about outside of work and start dreaming together about the possibilities.

If you are wondering how to go about getting everyone on board, why not try the action steps below. You never know what it may spark!

1. Ask your team members to each bring one big idea to the table – something that they would love to support or be involved in, regardless of cost.

2. Ask everyone to bring one community idea to the table – something that you could support immediately to make a difference to the lives of people in your locality.

3. Start with a round-table discussion of all the ideas and settle on two – three concepts in each category as agreed on by the group.

4. Run a 'Make Me Better' session for each of the remaining ideas where staff can contribute to the development of plans and strategies.

5. Aim to have one local community plan and one big idea that looks way beyond your immediate sphere of influence.

Have fun with it! This is a terrific opportunity to build relationships within your team as you embark on the adventure of a lifetime.

CHAPTER EIGHT

The next steps

WHERE TO FROM HERE?

We are nearly at the end of our journey. My hope and prayer is that you have been inspired to embrace the generous culture of caring, sharing and prosperity for all. For too long, we have accepted the status quo and assumed that a culture based on greed, fear and corruption is the only way. That is a lie. If you take nothing else away from our time together, challenge the culture and explore the alternatives for yourself.

Do you remember our starting point? I asked a question. Why does business ultimately exist? I believe with all my heart that all businesses exist to prosper and provide for the welfare of the whole of society, and I hope that I have gone some way to convince you that it's the best way to do life and business.

Life is about relationships. In the end, your possessions won't remember you fondly or talk about the impact you had on them. Money is a resource that we need to steward wisely and use for the benefit of ourselves, our families, businesses, communities and beyond. For me, the most important relationship is the one

I have with God. It's this relationship, with Jesus Christ, God the Father and the Holy Spirit that informs every other connection. As somebody who met Jesus at the age of twenty-seven, I can say without a shadow of a doubt that He changed my life for the better in every way.

He is the one who ultimately deserves the credit for any insight I've gained into business culture. As I've written this book, I've recognised the pattern more clearly than ever before. My revelation moments in business have always been preceded by the Lord putting His finger lovingly on the part of my life that's not working as He designed. Without exception, it's as I've said "Yes" to His call to upgrade that the downloads have arrived.

What I really want you to get is that He didn't wait for the work in me to be complete before downloading revelation. He doesn't require us to have it all together before revealing more. I love that about Him. He works with us in our mess and is apparently delighted to do so!

Your business and life are about more than you. If you have been blessed with the opportunity to own and run a business, don't take it for granted. Take time to consider the world around you. The more I have lifted my eyes from my circumstances to recognise the needs of others, the richer my life has become.

I have aimed to provoke your thinking, using my life as an example, and giving steps that you can take today to transform the culture of your business or workplace to one of generosity. I've shared my triumphs and failures so that you can avoid rein-venting the wheel and successfully navigate the pitfalls that come with this new territory.

It's about legacy. What do you want to leave behind? How do you want to be remembered? I want to be remembered as someone who championed others and lived generously. I want people to come first; before task, before profit. I want as many people as possible to benefit from the experiences I've had and the lessons I've learned. Above all, I want to be known, while I'm alive, as somebody who says "Yes" to God.

Businesses need healing. The people in them need healing from the wounds inflicted over generations by a culture of greed, fear and corruption. You have the opportunity to unlock and unleash the creative potential of your team. No one person has all the answers, and as leaders, it's in the best interests of our companies to commit to calling up the gold residing in people we rub shoulders with every day.

I believe that transforming toxic cultures is an idea whose time has come. When we're released from the need to win at all costs, we can look up, look around and consider others. When a win for others is a win for all, it takes power away from a system that seeks to divide and conquer. Together, we can rehabilitate businesses. Together, we can rehabilitate and restore the world, and united, we can rehabilitate the environment.

So, how are you doing with all of this transformational talk? You may be inspired. You may be scared. You may feel overwhelmed. You may think that none of this applies to you because you are a sole trader operating out of your spare bedroom. Or maybe you look around your company of two-hundred employees and the thought of trying to change the culture makes you shudder!

You can do it! If I did, you can too. If you want to see change, you will have to own your stuff (if I haven't said that enough!) and cultivate the grace and patience required to let others do the same. I won't pretend it's easy; but when is anything worth anything easy?

We are the revolutionaries. We are the pioneers. We dare to point out that the emperor has no clothes! More than that, we come with solutions based on love and generosity. We work with the original design for the world instead of the culture superimposed when humanity decided to do life based on our ability to navigate good and evil.

Revisit this book as often as you need. I'm not giving you a quick fix solution. You'll need to take stock of your life as much as your business. Transitioning from fear to favour is very much contingent on you being willing to own your stuff and work on it!

This chapter is about the 'Next Steps', so let's recap some of the immediate steps you can take to begin to transform the culture of your business and move from fear to outrageous favour.

1. Get copies of *Take Your Framework and Stick It Up Your Pipeline* for your staff/co-workers/boss and read it as a company!

2. Challenge the toxic culture of greed, fear and corruption by coming to the table in the spirit of generosity.

3. Talk with your staff about a culture of caring, sharing and prosperity for all and find out what that looks like for others.

4. Take the 'Tombstone Test'.

5. Spend time defining 'success' and 'failure' on both a personal level and for your business.

6. Make it your mission to catch people in the act of doing things right!

7. Discuss your 'Why', 'What', 'How' and 'Who' firstly with your leadership team. If you have vision and mission statements, review them and be honest about whether or not they fit a culture of generosity.

8. Get your hands on *The Big Five for Life* by John Strelecky and have your company read it.

9. Use the Action Steps in each chapter of this book to take your team on the journey from fear to outrageous favour!

10. Check out Transformational Leadership and consider attending an event in your area or joining the online community.

Remember that it will take some time to build trust with your team around this stuff. Keep the lines of communication open. This is the time to be dangerously transparent. Again, it's about coming in the opposite spirit. The traditional business culture brings with it levels of control and requires varying degrees of secrecy. Let's flip it!

For me, operating with dangerous transparency has only been possible because I know that I am fully known and fully loved by God. Connecting with the source of unconditional love and forgiveness has been THE key for me in this whole journey. It's God who protects my heart and sets the direction for my life, and in that I am secure. I want you to have that. More than anything else, I want that for you.

God knows you, and He loves you. He wants to have a relationship with you and reveal the plans and purposes in His heart for you. You have a destiny that is meant to change the world around you. That is what it means to bring Heaven to Earth, and no one is left out.

> For the anxious longing of the creation waits eagerly for the revealing of the sons of God. Romans 8:19 New American Standard Bible (NASB)

The world groans in waiting for us to step up and be all that He made us to be. We have the answer. He is the answer.

As I've said throughout the book, if you don't yet have a relationship with Jesus Christ, I want to invite you to give Him a go. What have you got to lose by asking Him into your life? I promise you that nothing compares to His love. Once you have His perspective on life, the world will open up in ways you never thought possible. Imagine dreaming with the creative force behind the universe!

This song, written a few thousand years ago by King David, sums it up.

YOU KNOW ALL ABOUT ME

For the Pure and Shining One
King David's poetic song

Lord, you know everything there is to know about me.
You perceive every movement of my heart and soul,
and you understand my every thought before it even enters
my mind.
You are so intimately aware of me, Lord.
You read my heart like an open book
and you know all the words I'm about to speak
before I even start a sentence!
You know every step I will take before my journey even begins.
You've gone into my future to prepare the way,

and in kindness you follow behind me
to spare me from the harm of my past.
With your hand of love upon my life,
you impart a blessing to me.
This is just too wonderful, deep, and incomprehensible!
Your understanding of me brings me wonder and strength.
Where could I go from your Spirit?
Where could I run and hide from your face?
If I go up to Heaven, you're there!
If I go down to the realm of the dead, you're there too!
If I fly with wings into the shining dawn, you're there!
If I fly into the radiant sunset, you're there waiting!
Wherever I go, your hand will guide me;
your strength will empower me.
It's impossible to disappear from you
or to ask the darkness to hide me,
for your presence is everywhere, bringing light into my night.
There is no such thing as darkness with you.
The night, to you, is as bright as the day;
there's no difference between the two.
You formed my innermost being, shaping my delicate inside
and my intricate outside,
and wove them all together in my mother's womb.
I thank you, God, for making me so mysteriously complex!
Everything you do is marvelously breathtaking.
It simply amazes me to think about it!
How thoroughly you know me, Lord!
You even formed every bone in my body
when you created me in the secret place,
carefully, skillfully shaping me from nothing to something.
You saw who you created me to be before I became me!
Before I'd ever seen the light of day,

the number of days you planned for me
were already recorded in your book.
Every single moment you are thinking of me!
How precious and wonderful to consider
that you cherish me constantly in your every thought!
O God, your desires toward me are more
than the grains of sand on every shore!
When I awake each morning, you're still with me.
Psalm 139: 1-18 The Passion Translation (TPT)

Finally, I strongly encourage you to look up, look around and consider how you can change the lives of people in your community and beyond. It might be as simple as connecting with your local sporting club and finding out what they need. It could be organising a working bee to help with gardening for older members of the community. Find out what your staff are passionate about, you never know what incredible adventures it may launch your business on!

Thank you for investing your time and energy in reading this book. I pray that you, your business, your staff, clients, family and friends prosper and in so doing, move from fear to outrageous favour. May the culture of generosity be evident in all you do and may you be fearless forerunners who tear down the toxic culture of greed, fear and corruption and replace it with generosity, caring, sharing and prosperity for all!

Blessings

Hugh Marquis

Notes

Chapter One

Stone, O. (Director). (1987). *Wall Street* [Motion Picture].

McCrindle. (2018). *McCrindle Small Business Research 2018*. Retrieved from McCrindle: https://mcrindle.com.au/wp-content/uploads/2018/04/Australia-Small-Business-Nation_McCrindle-Research.pdf

U.S. Small Business Administration Office of Advocacy. (2018). *Frequently Asked Questions About Small Business*. Retrieved from U.S. Small Business Administration Office of Advocacy: https://www.sba.gov/sites/default/files/advocacy/Frequently-Asked-Questions-Small-Business-2018.pdf

Chapter Two

Strelecky, J. (2007, 2012). *Big Five for Life*. Windermere, FL: Aspen Light Publishing (Kindle Edition).

Chapter Three

Strelecky, J. (2007, 2012). *Big Five for Life*. Windermere, FL: Aspen Light Publishing (Kindle Edition).

Warren, R. (2002). *The Purpose Driven Life: What On Earth Am I Here For?* Grand Rapids, Michigan: Zondervan.

Whyte, W. (1950). Is Anybody Listening? *Fortune, Time Inc.*, 77-174.

Cooke, G. (2017). *Greater Than Life Quotes*. Retrieved from Greater Than Life: http://greaterthan.life/graham-cooke-quotes/

DeMoss, N., and Grissom, T. (2004). Proud People, Humble People. *Seeking Him: Experiencing the Joy of Personal Revival.* United States of America: Moody Publishers.

Chapter Four

dictionary.com. (2018). *Expectation. (n.d.) retrieved from dictionary.com/browse/expectation.* Retrieved from dictionary.com: https://www.dictionary.com/browse/expectation

Zenger, J., and Folkman, J. (2015, March 15). 'The Ideal Praise to Criticism'. Retrieved from *Harvard Business Review*: https://hbr.org/2013/03/the-ideal-praise-to-criticism

Chapter Five

Cairnes, R. (2018, June 28). 'Here's why you're better off retraining employees than hiring new staff'. Retrieved from *Business Insider*: https://www.businessinsider.com.au/heres-why-youre-better-off-retraining-employees-than-hiring-new-staff-2018-6

REBBL. (2019). *Our Story.* Retrieved from REBBL: https://rebbl.co/our-story/

Brown, B. (2018). *Dare to Lead.* Ebury Digital (Kindle Edition).

Chapter Six

They Did Not Fail. (2018). *They Did Not Fail.* Retrieved from They Did Not Fail: https://www.uky.edu/~eushe2/Pajares/OnFailingG.html

McHugh, P. (2002). *You and the Creative Force of Frustration.* Box Hill, Victoria: The Hanerda Trust.

Chapter Seven

Warren, R. (2002). *The Purpose Driven Life: What On Earth Am I Here For?* Grand Rapids, Michigan: Zondervan.

About the author

Hugh is married to Jane, and they have three grown children, Breanne, Savannah, and Owen. Hugh has been building and running successful (and the odd not-so-successful) businesses for thirty-two years. He's run restaurants, bars, hotels and French bakehouses. He's built and renovated houses, developed properties, written computer software, worked in finance, built IT service businesses, and developed multimillion-dollar enterprises all around the world.

Hugh and Jane run organisations tackling human trafficking and slavery in Cambodia and other developing nations. In their pursuit to end human trafficking, they realised that they must work upstream and solve the root cause. They are committed to releasing people in business into the fullness of their purpose to provide for and prosper the whole of society. While they call Melbourne, Australia home, Hugh and Jane travel extensively world-wide teaching, equipping and releasing leaders across business and churches to do Kingdom business.